GARDEN

GARDEN
RANDLE SIDDELEY

Text by Helen Chislett

'Lighting the Garden' by Sally Storey

F

FRANCES LINCOLN LIMITED
PUBLISHERS

I would like to dedicate this book to my family: to my father, John Siddeley, who passed on his passion for excellence in design and who commissioned the first two landscape projects on which my business was founded. To my mother, Jacqueline, for creating an environment for me to grow up in which nurtured my interest and enthusiasm for gardens. To my wife, Kiki, who has for years patiently put up with me being in foreign climes, often at short notice and at the most inconvenient times. And to William and Edward, who I hope will one day have gardens to love of their own.

PAGE 1: A series of wide steps lead to the main terrace of a country house in Quebec.
PAGES 2–3: Lawns, lakes and trees complement the graceful architecture of this magnificent Georgian house in the English countryside.
BELOW: A contemporary garden pavilion makes a focal point in this sumptuous city garden.

CONTENTS

FOREWORD

The older I get, the more I appreciate the enormous care and attention that goes into creating a garden of distinction. Gardens are often described as outdoor rooms – and it is true that the best ones are a natural extension of the house – but a garden designer has so much more to think about than an interior designer. When you decorate a room inside, the paint goes on the walls and the effect is instant. In a garden, it may take years before the vision of the designer becomes reality. Garden design is not just about creating something pretty on paper but about understanding how views will change over seasons and time; how high plants and trees will grow; the relationship and the harmony between flowers; and how the garden will look in two years' time – and twenty. There are other challenges, too, not least that of understanding how people will use the garden and how it will be maintained. There is no point in creating something wonderful that will take many man hours to keep up unless the owner is committed to that fact in the long run.

I love gardens that are beautiful in their simplicity, such as the White Garden at Sissinghurst in Kent or the herbaceous borders at Hidcote Manor in Gloucestershire. My own garden in Provence is mainly box hedging, roses and lavender; not only does it look wonderful, but it sits perfectly in its environment. This idea of designing a garden that fits with its landscape is central to the best of garden design. A landscape designer may be skilled at taming nature – digging lakes, moving trees, terracing hills – but a good one will never fight her.

Looking through the gardens of Randle Siddeley, I see the eye of a great artist at work. I share his love of wildness juxtaposed with structure, of textural contrasts within planting and of water features large and small. Each garden is a canvas – some enormous, some tiny – on to which he imprints a design that looks as though it must always have been there. We see only the glorious results and not the poor soil, unfriendly climate, unpromising space, diggers (both machine and human) or once-empty flower beds. It takes great confidence and enormous passion to see a garden through from first stages to full flourish. Garden design is a cocktail of knowledge, skill, love and faith. It seems to me that Randle has all of these in abundance.

David Linley

A line of clipped cypress trees punctuates the olive trees and lavender terraces on this idyllic estate in the south of France with its backdrop of parasol pines.

INTRODUCTION

8   When I was a child, I was lucky enough always to have wonderful outdoor spaces to play in. My parents lived in London during the week, but at weekends and holidays we would decamp to the Suffolk countryside. In the first house I lived in, Old Oak Cottage, my bedroom was on the ground floor, so when I was very young I could actually clamber out of the window into the garden when nobody else was yet awake and enjoy it all to myself. I had a small plot of my own in the kitchen garden and that is where I would go to tend my marigolds, nasturtiums, Sweet Williams and wallflowers. I rather overdosed on all those bright colours, but I was very dyslexic as a child and being able to see results from the seeds I planted compensated hugely for the problems I encountered with reading and writing. I realized that a garden allows you to escape and to create your own world.

We later moved to a house called The Deans, which had a huge garden of about 3.5 hectares/9 acres. There were glorious herbaceous borders, a wildflower garden, a walled garden and, my father's pride and joy, the rose garden. My father, the interior designer John Siddeley, was passionate about growing roses and he cultivated hundreds of long-stemmed beauties, which he would pack into the car every Sunday evening during the summer months to deliver to Pulbrook & Gould in Chelsea early the next morning. His reasoning was that this extra income paid for the gardener, but in truth he just loved growing roses.

The gardener, Mr Buckledy, was a great influence on me. I also had my own small plot of garden at The Deans, and Mr Buckledy was a mine of garden information, who never seemed to mind having a child – me – following him around asking question after question. As I have often said to my clients, without the person who looks after the garden, we are at a loss.

There was a garden nursery near by, Crampthorne's, where my father bought a lot of plants. As a teenager, I worked there in my holidays and learnt many horticultural skills such as grafting and pruning. I also had holiday jobs at Pulbrook & Gould, where I met the wonderful Anne Orde – then the company's head florist and a talented plantswoman. When I began my own company some years later, Anne worked with me for the first few years, passing on a huge amount of plant knowledge which significantly increased my confidence.

During my thirty-five years in the landscape business, I have seen big changes both in working practices and in how the industry is perceived.

I like to think I have been influential in being part of that change. When I started out, there was no design-and-build. I was the first to see there was a synergy between the two stages, and that rather than rely on a sub-contractor to implement a design well, it made more sense to take responsibility for a garden's creation from concept to installation and – where appropriate – maintenance.

Although I was passionately interested in gardens from an early age, I actually began my professional life working for my father, so I speak from experience when I say that designing a garden presents significant additional challenges to those of renovating a home. With interior design, you can see fairly instantly whether a particular paint colour works or whether a sofa is in the right place. With gardens, you have to wait months – sometimes years – to see whether the effect you planned has been achieved. The other problem is that whereas rooms, if left, remain static, a garden is always changing. It might look exactly as you wanted it to at the end of a year, but you can't freeze it in time. That is why all gardens are really a work in progress. Finally, if you do get it wrong, it is very, very expensive to put a garden right.

As a garden designer, I also find my clients are not nearly so confident in expressing their opinions about their gardens as they might be about their houses. The very fact that plants have formal Latin names is enough to intimidate them. I spend a lot of time at the beginning of a project encouraging clients to think about what they want from the garden and about gardens they themselves have visited and liked. Being a good designer does not mean imposing my signature on someone else's garden; it means trying to ensure that the people we work for end up with the garden they really want.

Of course there are many individual choices that go into a garden design – everything from which sort of paving to use to how best to frame a view – but when I first step into the garden it is not with these specifics in mind. The first things that hit me are the vertical and the horizontal lines. At their simplest these could be the trees and the hedges, but in fact the more you

In the south of France, a suspended walkway through woodland punctuated with parasol pines leads to a vantage point where views to the sea and hills can be enjoyed.

10 look, the more you will see that all landscapes are in effect a criss-cross of lines. When I design a garden, I am building on to that idea. Gardens must have structure, a backbone; like a house, they should comprise walls, roof, floor and windows. There are all kinds of ways you can create this underlying structure. Walls might be hedging, brick, fence or pergola; the roof may be the tops of trees or the rising of a terrace; floors could be hard paving or soft lawn; windows are the views you create, punctuated by water, sculpture or other special touches. I believe there should always be an element of mystery in a garden: allow the eye to see 70 per cent, not the whole 100 per cent. You want to turn a corner and come across something unexpected and beautiful, even in a modest-sized town garden.

Over the course of my working life, I have had the pleasure of designing many gardens of all sizes, locations and budgets. I have had wonderful clients, many of whom have asked me to create new gardens for them as they have moved from property to property. The gardens you will find in these pages may have begun with my design vision, but without a whole team of experts to turn those ideas into reality there would be nothing to see of any merit. I have been fortunate enough to work with exceptionally talented people, to whom I owe a great deal.

Since boyhood, I have seen the happiness that gardens give, a reward for all the patience and hard labour they entail. I think their enduring popularity is to do with what I first discovered at Old Oak Cottage: that sense of creating your own private world. For anyone who desires to do that for themselves, I hope this book will be both a guide and a friend.

Randle Siddeley

This bird's-eye view of a city roof terrace garden shows how space has been cleverly manipulated to provide zones for cooking, dining and relaxing.

THE PERFECT ENGLISH GARDEN

'It takes a designer's eye to see the potential of a garden like this, but bringing it to fruition means men, machines and a certain amount of mayhem. You have to keep telling yourself it will all be worth it and keep the faith.'

This is a small, private estate which stretches along a steeply banked Cotswold valley. The clients use the handsome Grade II-listed Edwardian house as a weekend retreat for themselves, their children and their friends. The garden is enormous – about 3.5 hectares/9 acres in all, including ancient beech woodland.

Originally instructed to landscape around the house itself, Randle advocated the need for a more ambitious and comprehensive master plan, which would give the vast area a sense of structure and release the garden's true potential.

FAR LEFT: Potted miniature topiary on the dining table makes a witty visual link to the mature topiary specimens beyond.

LEFT: An inviting and unusual circular swing makes good use of an existing cedar of Lebanon tree at the front of the house.

RIGHT: A classic, ornate eighteenth-century pedestal-mounted stone urn makes a striking statement at the intersection of two walkways.

CHALLENGE

This was a house that was completely lacking a formal garden to walk around and enjoy. The gardens sloped down to the property, overshadowing it, and there was an uninteresting view from the house to a vegetable garden. A high bank of grass to the rear meant that there was no room for an *al fresco* dining area.

VISION

Randle could immediately see the possibilities of a complete transformation of the outside space. He planned a new layout that would be terraced into different garden rooms, with a secluded and luxurious swimming-pool area at the top of the garden looking out over the wonderful views. He also allowed for a generous circular dining area to be cut into the lawn, close to the house. This would be paved in York stone, complemented by clipped box shapes in attractive clay planters.

SOLUTION

This was a major earth-moving exercise that took over four years to complete. First of all, the high bank to the back of the house was pushed back, allowing the dining area to be created. Then an intensive 'cut and fill' operation was

ABOVE: Randle designed this circular stone dining area to be cut into the lawn. A stone path on which topiary plants are positioned accentuates the undulations of the terraces beyond.
RIGHT: Standard olive trees at the corners of the swimming pool make a visual link to the line of pleached lime trees that delineate this part of the garden from the rest.

initiated on the planned pool site, later extended to create 0.8 hectares/2 acres of level garden from what had been an unpromising slope. Tons of Cotswold stone were excavated and then used to rebuild existing walls and act as retainers on new ones. These walls were of paramount importance, because they provided support for the new terraces. New walls in the swimming-pool area were camouflaged with crescents of pleached lime trees.

Once the main structure was created, two gardens of contrasting mood and character were planted: an orchard with a wildflower meadow, and a formal rose garden. Down one side of the latter is a pergola of oak, festooned with swags of climbing roses, while architectural obelisks provide support for more roses. The two gardens are linked by an area of silver birch and pine trees, in sympathy with the woodland that surrounds the property. The series of newly constructed terraces incorporates three tiers of traditional fruit trees, with banks of wild flowers descending to the house. In addition, Randle created a romantic woodland garden, carpeted with wild flowers, and a children's 'secret' garden.

PLANTING

The clients had requested that the garden be at its peak

LEFT: Paths of stone and gravel lead the eye through traditionally romantic planting, punctuated by clipped yew, to the magnificent rose garden beyond.

ABOVE: Randle created a spring-time wonderland by planting thousands of bulbs and wildflowers in the banks bordering the driveway.

FOLLOWING PAGES: The spectacular rose garden is the centrepiece of Randle's design. Obelisks add structure, while an abundance of herbaceous varieties complement the palette of roses.

in July and August. Their preference was for soft whites, pinks and blues, rather than hot reds or yellows. Randle kept the planting schemes relatively simple: late-flowering, traditional roses for the enchanting and romantic rose garden, mixed with a wide variety of herbaceous plants including artemisia, lavatera, scabious, salvias, hyssop, astrantia, plenty of lavender varieties and agapanthus, all set off by dramatically shaped yew topiary. He also introduced thousands of spring-flowering bulbs along the existing driveway, with a scattering of white Shasta daisies and wild barley. Around the pool, he created an informal planting scheme of stipa grasses, white aquilegia, thalictrum and more agapanthus.

RESULT

This is a garden for which the clients had low expectations, but which they now passionately love and use as often as possible. Visitors are captivated by its many levels and rooms, while friends and family make full use of the swimming pool and the *al fresco* dining area, and enjoy the garden's many charms. As the planting matures, their pleasure increases year on year.

'When you disrupt the landscape to this extent, cutting down into the bedrock, you have to allow time for everything to settle again before planting. It is no different to going through a complicated and dramatic operation, from which it takes time to recover. All gardeners set out to control nature, but you have to respect it too – ensuring the land drains properly, for example, is crucial. Also, planting trees is one thing, but you also have to make sure that each specimen has sufficient space to thrive and grow. It wasn't until about the fourth year that the yew planting here started to establish itself, but now it looks as though it has been there for ever. Establishing a garden of this scale properly cannot be rushed; with schemes like this clients have to understand they are in it for the long term.'

ABOVE: This pergola of oak and swagged rope, thick with Dublin Bay climbing roses, has been softened with lavender bushes planted at the base of each support.
RIGHT: A weeping ash is the pivotal feature of the central circular bed in the rose garden – an informal contrast to the more architectural wooden obelisks.

DESIGN

I came into garden design having studied architecture and having been brought up with a background of interior design through my father. He believed, rightly, that a good designer should understand the construction of a house and everything that went on behind its walls. Because of this, I spent time apprenticed to plumbers, joiners, electricians, decorators – every aspect of the building industry. I worked in furniture factories and fabric mills. I spent each holiday with one of my father's various contractors, learning different trades. It was an extraordinary learning curve.

The same thing applies to landscape design. It is not enough to select plants or choose the right colour of stone: you have to understand aspect, light, climate, soil, water tables and wind direction. You have to be able to look beyond what is there and see how something radically different might work. You have to feel a sympathy with the setting of the house and garden, with the architecture and age of the building, with the people whose garden this is. Then you have to work within constraints of budget and time to achieve a magical result. If I have one golden rule it is: don't rush. Time spent really getting to know a garden and seeing how it changes from season to season will make all the difference to the success of a design. Structure is the backbone of a garden; once this is in place, all the other ingredients of a beautiful garden follow so much more easily.

DESIGNING YOUR OWN GARDEN

If you want a really spectacular garden, the first thing to suggest is that you will probably need help. A garden designer is trained to see all the potential within a given space, and will understand both how to make the best of its finer features and how to distract the eye from its unsightly ones. In addition, he or she will understand the capabilities of the garden in terms of soil construction, the movement of light and how trees and shrubs will change according to the seasons. This will guide the designer towards creating a planting scheme that will not only be beautiful to look at but will also thrive in those surroundings.

You can take many years to create the garden of your dreams, but the important thing is to have a master plan to work from. Even if this is all you can afford to do at the moment, it will be money well spent. A master plan first needs a technical survey; this will provide the designer with a drawing of the garden to scale, showing boundaries, any permanent features, contours, levels and so forth. A good designer will then talk to you at length about what you most want from your garden, in terms of both function and aesthetics.

Your chosen designer should ask you a lot of questions about what you want from the garden in terms of practicality (see the checklist opposite): who is going to use it, when will it be most used, what it will be used for and so on. It is also helpful if you can sort out priorities: a vegetable garden, for example, may be at the very top of your own list, whereas your partner may be dreaming of a new driveway and your children of a tree house. With the designer's help, you should be able to decide the order in which work should be done. There is no point planting a beautiful lawn if in two years' time you are planning to drive heavy machinery over it to build a gazebo.

There is often a misunderstanding about gardens compared to houses: people expect their construction to be simpler. In fact they are equally complicated. Just as you would not hang the curtains and then decide to do the rewiring or replumbing, so in a garden you have to make sure that all your essential services are in place before you begin planting. The garden designer may well recommend that you budget for a lighting designer from the start, because lighting has an incredible impact. It not only allows you to extend the hours for which you use a garden – maximizing your enjoyment of it – but it also brings atmosphere, interest and personality into your outdoor space. You may not be able to afford all the lighting features you would like at the very beginning, but you want to have all the cables laid so that it is easy to add lighting features at a later date.

Once you have essential services in the right positions and have agreed a logical order and timescale for the garden's transformation, you can begin to tackle questions of style, with your designer's help: type of boundary (wall, fence, hedge); size, style and colour of hard surfaces (paving stones, decking, gravel), planting schemes . . . Again there is a parallel with interior design: boundaries are the walls;

hard surfaces the floors; planting schemes the soft furnishings.

A competent garden designer will encourage you to view your garden as a series of rooms, rather than one big space. There are decisions to be made not only about how you access the garden from different points of the house but about how you travel around the garden; the connection of different levels and different 'rooms'; the enjoyment of views in all directions; the change of surfaces underfoot to signify a different mood; the focal points within a space, be they natural ones such as mature trees or man-made ones such as sculpture or gazebos. Even a tiny garden needs careful consideration in order to 'zone' it appropriately – where is the seating area, the visual interest, the traffic route?

Be bold and brave when it comes to the design of your garden. Too often people get locked into certain ideas, because these reflect the way the garden has always looked: a terrace by the house, a bit of lawn, some flower beds. You may think you want to keep the essential structure of your garden and simply ask a designer to refresh it in some way. But if he or she sees other possibilities, a way of reconfiguring the space to improve both the way it is used and the way it looks, open your mind to their suggestions. Many of the gardens shown here began with a request from a client for me to pep the garden up in some way but resulted in my overseeing their total transformation. The most successful schemes are probably those where a designer is able to strip out everything (except protected trees) and begin again – a blank canvas. You have to trust the eye of the professional you have hired. Landscape designers spend many years learning their craft; they will be more able than you are to see what could be created within the given space.

If the basic design of the garden is done well, it is always possible to change its character and mood with different planting over the seasons. Again this is not dissimilar to designing a house, where the core scheme can be reinvigorated with different combinations of cushions, curtains and accessories. With a strong structure in place, it is down to you how to 'dress' the garden with flowers and foliage.

A well-designed garden should not shriek of the designer's input. If

CHECKLIST

These are the sorts of questions a garden designer should ask you:

- Who is going to use this garden (adults, children, animals)?
- At what times of the year and day will it be used most?
- Which activities will take place here (e.g. eating, playing, sunbathing, swimming)?
- What do you like most about it?
- What do you dislike most about it?
- Are privacy and security an issue?
- What is on your own wish list and that of your family?
- Which styles of garden do you like? (Tear sheets and books are useful to give an idea.)
- What is the timescale? (This can be years.)
- What is the budget? (Be honest – there's no point in stating a figure that is in fact unachievable.)
- How will it be maintained? (By yourself or staff?)
- How much time will be available for its maintenance?

Other points to discuss include:

- Whether there are protected trees or Listed Building requirements.
- Views – both those you want to lose and those you want to make more of, including 'borrowed' views over neighbouring properties.
- Safety – particularly where children are concerned (from water, roads, etc.).
- The age and architecture of the house – house and garden need to sit happily with each other.
- Unsightly but necessary features that need camouflaging in some way.
- Drainage – often overlooked, but it is essential that water drains away easily and does not cause lawns to become boggy or plants saturated.

he or she has done the job well, it will appear to have always looked this beautiful – in tune with its location, the surrounding architecture and the landscape beyond. It will not just be something pretty to be viewed from the house: it will be a continuation of the house, a place where every member of the family has their own favourite corner. It will also be an investment, for great gardens add enormously to both the value and saleability of a property. However, the fact is that if you design a garden that is perfect for you, you will probably never want to move again.

MAINTENANCE

Just as a house needs to be cleaned, so a garden needs to be maintained. Paths need to be weeded, plants pruned, lawns cut. Be realistic about the hours you can afford to put into your garden or the help you will need. A design can always be simplified to meet your lifestyle, so be honest about this when talking to a garden designer. In many of the gardens I have designed, we have employed and trained a gardening team to continue our work. The implementation of a design is, after all, only the beginning.

VIEWS

If there is one thing that most people wish for from a garden, it is a fantastic view. Should you be fortunate enough to have a garden that enjoys a great aspect, you will want to do everything you can to frame the view and to make it part of the garden's character. Make sure that anything you plant will not block the views on maturity, and keep boundary hedges and suchlike well pruned.

Don't forget that it is also advisable to think of views and vistas within the garden. The best locations are ones that give the eye something beautiful to look at in the distance, but then the viewer's attention is captivated by other wonderful features within the garden itself. There is a sense of being seduced, of something happening beyond what can be clearly seen, so that you feel physically compelled to explore the garden further rather than simply look.

Stand back and look at your house, and consider what you can do to complement the architecture in terms of planting and landscaping. This applies both to the back of the house and to the front. If you have focal points, such as sculpture or water features, place them so that they have maximum impact. This doesn't necessarily mean placing them where they can be on view from the house; often it is better to turn a corner and happen across something amazing. Lighting can also be used to accentuate the effect. Works of art or magnificent specimen trees take on new resonance if dramatically lit when the rest of the garden is in darkness.

City dwellers should also remember the importance of borrowed views. Don't design a garden that entirely blocks out neighbouring properties – the chances are you will never manage to do this anyway; instead, think about how you can benefit from the trees and greenery that surround your property.

Finally, make sure that your garden design is in tune with the landscape around it. If you are lucky enough to have open views and big skies, a garden that is too fussy and fiddly will seems at odds with these. Your garden and the view beyond need to merge together seamlessly.

UGLY FEATURES

It is one thing to have a totally blank canvas on which to create a beautiful garden; it is quite another to inherit difficult and ugly features that somehow have to be assimilated into the design. One of the architectural curses of contemporary urban life, for example, is the subterranean extension – an underground swimming pool and recreation gym that often runs the length of a city garden and has ubiquitous curved skylights that resemble bulbous eye-balls. Of course they are not the only example: in city gardens, I have also had to contend with towering boundary walls, ventilation shafts, unwieldy changes of level and unsightly fire escapes. In the country, it is often a question of working around unattractive access roads, inauspicious farm buildings, pylons and paddock fencing.

Whatever the challenge your particular garden has thrown at you, the secret lies in drawing the eye away from the problem area and not towards it. The 'eye-ball' example I gave is typical. No amount of box hedging and lavender is going to transform something so fundamentally ugly into something beautiful. Better to look at ways of screening off such an unattractive necessity and instead creating focal points elsewhere, such as a fabulous water feature. Within these pages, there are many examples of gardens that presented huge problems in terms of permanent structures, but the flip side to that coin is that often they inspired the greatest creativity.

The art is in creating different views, even in small gardens, that distract attention from the fixed objects you can do little about. At the stage when you have stripped out a garden in order to begin imposing a new design, it can be disheartening to be faced with a dominating and unattractive feature. However, once your new garden has matured, you will see how well this approach works – get the design right and the eye simply fails to register it.

CHILDREN

Gardens are a huge part of children's lives. They are a playground, a make-believe land, a nature safari, a picnic place. They don't need Wendy houses, tree houses, climbing frames, tennis courts or swimming pools, but if you have room for any of these, children will exert enormous pressure to get them – and often they succeed. The trick of designing a garden around a family is to look ahead. A toddler will be happy with a sandpit and paddling pool on the terrace, but it won't be long before he or she wants swings, slides, somewhere to ride his or her bike and some kind of den. It doesn't end there. My own two sons have taken over our garden for football, cricket, ping-pong and every kind of sporting activity. And I haven't even mentioned pets . . .

So be practical. If your children are young, you need to know they are always close to the house, well contained and easy to supervise. Clear sight lines from the house to the play area are essential. But as they grow older, you might do better to create a space for them that is further from the house, where they can be as messy and noisy as they like. Safety is paramount, though. Swimming-pool areas should always

be secure and lockable; ponds and rills are best avoided until children are of an age when there is no chance of them accidentally falling in; and the same goes for the water troughs that often form a part of ornamental water features.

If you have children who are mad on games, such as football, rounders or cricket, it is probably best simply to accept that you will have to postpone your dreams of a Sissinghurst-style garden until they leave home! Sow grass that can withstand tough usage and don't waste money on delicate plants that risk being crushed by stray balls. There is no point stressing out your children and yourself by fretting over the state of the lawn.

However, just as within the house you probably have one area that is adult friendly, make sure you keep one area of the garden primarily for your own use and enjoyment – even if it is the place where you grow vegetables. Gardens are a joyful place for children, but they should be a pleasure to everyone in the family.

THE NEW-BUILD GARDEN

As a landscape designer, I am usually asked to remodel an existing garden or at the very least find a way of breathing new interest into an existing layout. However, there are many occasions when I am asked to create a garden for a new-build home, which can be an exciting opportunity to see a design through from a skeleton structure to maturity. Of course that isn't to say that there is nothing in place already. Some of my clients are lucky enough to build their dream homes in landscapes rich in trees, lakes and views, but where the countryside has never yet been tamed into formal gardens.

The two gardens I have selected here could not be more different: a huge country estate in Canada and an urban home in the Middle East. The first was almost Versailles-style in its ambition: a magnificent new mansion in dramatic mountain scenery that I first glimpsed from the client's helicopter. A wealth of indigenous trees, such as pine, silver birch and aspen, surrounding it offered the perfect backdrop to a formal garden of terraces, lawns and classical references. The second was more typical of the challenges of a new build: a compact space, overlooked by other buildings, which demanded a garden that was functional and fun, but also highly individual.

What connects them is the idea that design is not something imposed without empathy on to a piece of land but is rather a force that harnesses climate, environment and surrounding architecture to create a garden that is absolutely right for its location.

A statue of Thomas Jefferson stands in the centre of the Jefferson garden, one of a series of gardens Randle created for clients in Quebec with a backdrop of herbaceous planting and a yew hedge. This leads up to the carefully disguised main driveway.

THE BIG PICTURE

'There are people who talk about things and there are people, like my clients, who have a dream and commit to making it happen. Transforming a space in such a spectacular way gives a great deal of pleasure both to the client and myself, but it has to be remembered that I am like the conductor of the orchestra: originating a design is one thing, but putting it into practice only works if you have the right team to help you, as I did here.'

It is not often that a landscape designer is given a domestic project to work on that is truly grand in scale. Randle was introduced to these Canadian clients at a point when they had recently built a new country home, in palatial Franco-Russian style, on their estate in Quebec. The house sits on a hill in dramatic mountainous scenery between two lakes surrounded by woodland and parkland, with its own golf course. Some formal gardens, including rose and parterre gardens, had already been added around the house, but nothing of sufficient splendour for such a magnificent location and style of building.

LEFT: A swimming pool blends into the architectural structure of the formal terraces that surround this neo-classical house.
ABOVE: The house nestles in its own paradise. Rising on the left is the music pavilion.

CHALLENGE

Weather was one of the biggest hurdles to overcome. On Randle's first site visit, there was snow 2–3 metres/7–10 feet deep, making it difficult to pace out the land properly and understand the contours or even locate the edges. Climate was also a big factor in deciding on the planting: winters here can drop to temperatures as low as –40°C/ –40°F with icy winds, and climb to 30–40°C/86–104°F in the hottest summers. Snow begins in October and continues until March or April, so the flowering period is very short – about four months between May and September, when everything flowers intensively. This is also the period when it is necessary to carry out essential maintenance work, before severe weather sets in once more.

This was a project on a huge scale – about 8 hectares/20 acres of formal gardens, set in an estate of many tens of thousands of acres. It is very unusual in this locality to have a garden in such a traditional style. Randle recognized that designing and creating such a garden was only one half of the story: he also had to ensure that it would be looked after

correctly and 'brought on' in his absence. To this purpose, the client employed a team of gardeners who undertook specialist training with Randle and his team when the latter were on site visits, so expanding their knowledge of – and therefore interest in – the garden. The training included instruction on growing plants from seed each winter, which would be ready for planting out the following summer. As well as greenhouses, hothouses had to be built that were large enough to accommodate citrus trees and other specimens that needed protection from the long, icy winters.

VISION

Randle realized that for such an impressive house set in a truly heart-jolting landscape, it was essential to create big vistas that would encompass the natural surroundings. As well as providing visual links between different areas of the estate, the design had to allow for the grandeur of the

ABOVE: Randle created this dramatic vista looking from the house up to the music pavilion. The gigantic terraces are camouflaged here by snow.
RIGHT: This long avenue of stone steps leads from the house to the main lake. The planting is carefully chosen to merge with the existing surroundings and is accentuated by shallow stone planters.

house itself to be appreciated. When he first visited, the house could not be seen from the driveway because it stood high on the hill, whereas the drive was accessed via a back road on a much lower level. It was necessary to manipulate the landscape to provide the grandiose backdrop that the house required. Around this, Randle planned a series of formal gardens, in keeping with the house's architectural inspiration, including an English rose garden.

SOLUTION

On Randle's first visit, he concentrated on the vista from the house to an ornate music pavilion that the clients had built on an adjacent hill. They had chiselled out a view of this by felling some trees, but Randle improved the effect considerably by having gigantic steps cut into the slope, forming terraces that lead the eye upwards. This was achieved through a significant amount of dynamiting and extensive use of heavy machinery. Specially constructed matting was used to hold

32

FAR LEFT: The formal gardens leading
up to the main house are protected by
high clipped hedges of thuja and avenues
of *Fraxinus excelsior*.
LEFT: One of the urns which Randle
replicated from the original, a late
eighteenth-century design from
Chateau de St Germain.

LEFT: These powerful sculptures by Ju Ming from the Taichi Series are the pivotal point between the formal avenue of stairs and the beautiful natural lake beyond.
RIGHT: Randle created this artist's impression of his vision for the vista, including the Ju Ming sculptures. The final result is almost identical.

everything in place, into which wildflower seeds were sown, with topsoil added. This method prevented the possibility of rock slippage destroying the terraces. The combination of native trees such as aspen, birch and pine, terraces planted with wild flowers, and plateaux of grass is truly spectacular. In addition, the garden around the music pavilion has been designed to be a flexible space to accommodate summer concerts.

The driveway was re-routed entirely on to a new access road. Now there are tantalizing glimpses of the house along the approach, but sometimes it drops mysteriously out of sight behind woodland, only to reappear again moments later from a new vantage point. This new route also offers wonderful views of the main lake, where Randle has created an island of rock taken from the estate quarry. A bold, monolithic sculpture by Ju Ming makes a powerful statement at the end of the parkland. The drive culminates in a circular area, set off by a magnificent antique urn of marble. Laser technology has been expertly used to clone this, providing four further urns that have been used in the parterre garden on the main terrace.

The rose garden has high hedges around it to protect it from the winds. A selection of roses complemented by herbaceous plants such as geraniums, hostas and alliums ensures that the garden is in glorious flower through the short summer with an eye-catching display of colour and

LEFT: Classical references abound throughout the property, complementing the architectural style of the house.
BELOW: Two classical pavilions mirror each other at the entrance to the Jefferson garden, a contrast to the wild landscape beyond.

DESIGN: THE NEW-BUILD GARDEN

LEFT: Top left: Contractors begin to take the design for the formal terraces from concept to reality.
Bottom left: Once all the architectural elements are in place, planting can follow.
Top right: With the obelisks positioned, it does not take long for plants to begin to flourish.
Bottom right: An eighteenth-century stone urn sets the classical tone.
RIGHT: A few seasons after being first planted, the terraces are already in a new stage of maturity and beauty.

texture. Randle's choice of architectural obelisks and trellises provides core structure and also makes a visual link to the group on the main terrace. Other garden areas include the Jefferson garden on the site of the former drive: named after Thomas Jefferson, this is themed around blues, whites and pinks. The parterre garden to the front of the house enjoys wonderful views to the second lake. A staircase of wide, shallow steps edged with planters leads from the house to the main lake.

PLANTING

Randle introduced a number of acid-soil-loving specimen trees and shrubs, including acers, magnolias, rhododendrons and azaleas. Ornamental grasses, such as *Sorghastrum nutans* and *Scizachyrium scoparium*, have been planted in drifts along the road that leads past the woodland area. The rose garden is planted with varieties such as 'Fragrant Cloud',

'Marie Bugnet' and 'Morden Snowbeauty'. Here 'Alburn' and 'Max Frei' geraniums are interplanted with hostas, irises, peonies, lilies, alchemilla, alliums and anemones. The parterre garden features box hedges, 'Hidcote' lavender, peonies, lilies, tulips and narcissus.

In the Jefferson garden, a life-size bronze of Thomas Jefferson is placed within a formal lawn surrounded by a high *Taxus cuspidata* and lime trees. Borders of lavender, agapanthus, and verbena give summer colour. A further lawn area leads from the Ju Ming sculpture down to the lake edge. Planting here is mainly informal sweeps of birches, acers and amelanchiers, with an underplanting of naturalized grasses, irises and ferns.

RESULT

The clients had the courage to support Randle's 'big vision' and gave him full rein to create the spectacular vistas he had

'Extreme temperatures such as those found in Canada are happily not the norm, but wherever you are it is important to understand how best to protect delicate plants over the winter period. If container-grown plants cannot be brought indoors, group them in a sheltered spot, with the most tender in the centre, making sure the containers stay as dry as possible. A covering of fleece will be of great benefit. You can also use fleece to wrap tropical plants, and to protect shrubs and small trees. Protect the crowns of herbaceous plants with a good layer of straw, oak leaves and mulch; don't fertilize them after August, so that they have time to get ready for the winter.'

envisaged. In an estate of many thousands of acres, there will be changes and improvements to be made for many years to come, so this is very much a work in progress. However, what has been achieved already far surpasses what they hoped for when they took the decision to build such a prestigious house. Joyfully, they describe the rose garden as their 'Monet garden'. While they take pleasure from Randle's designs, Randle takes pleasure from having clients who gave him the opportunity to flex his creative muscles on an epic scale.

ABOVE: A peaceful place to rest has been planted with many specimens including *Thalictrum aquilegiifolium*, *Veronicastrum virginicum*, *Nepeta* 'Kit Kat', *Hydrangea quercifolia* and *Salvia* 'May Night'.
RIGHT: The parterre garden to the front of the house features box hedging, lavender, helenium, lilies and guava.

COOL, CALM & CONTEMPORARY

'Having two or more distinct levels to a garden is always preferable to having a steep slope. Here I made sure the supporting walls were integrated into the design; at just 50 centimetres/20 inches high, they also provide extra comfortable seating. By making such a feature of the steps, accentuated by the flow of water from upper to lower levels, I ensured both parts of the garden worked in totality.'

This is a new-build home in the Middle East. The clients wanted to create a private oasis of calm in a bustling commercial city and, in such a warm climate, to maximize the possibility of outdoor living. The house is a landmark of architecture in the area, with a cool, contemporary interior designed by Kelly Hoppen. The clients wanted a garden that would be sympathetic to the design, without being overly minimalist.

FAR LEFT: The wall of water that Randle designed to provide screening from the adjacent property and create a dramatic backdrop to the front entrance of the house.
LEFT: Mature palm trees and a line of cypress trees were craned into the garden to provide instant landscaping.
ABOVE LEFT: The steps to the pool are edged with planters filled with frangipani (*Plumeria grandiflora*) and underplanted with *Impatiens balsamina* and *Lobelia erinus*.
ABOVE RIGHT: Cypress trees to the front of the house soften the rendered walls that border the entranceway. This wall has recessed lighting and hand-moulded brass leaf motifs.

CHALLENGE

The garden is about 0.2 hectares/half an acre in size, with houses encroaching on all sides. One priority was to screen these out as much as possible, giving a sense of privacy and intimacy. It was also necessary to link the house visually with the swimming-pool area, which is at a much lower level. All materials used had to be site specific, and so able to withstand the hot climate. It was also necessary to have someone on the team who could speak modern Hebrew, as well as working alongside a local landscape contractor who could advise on the suitability of plants.

VISION

In a relatively small garden, structure is particularly important, so Randle determined to introduce a line of mature palm trees to provide the spine of the garden. He was also inspired to design bespoke touches, such as a 4-metre/13-foot-high water feature to provide screening from the adjoining property when people enter the house, with a cascade of water making a theatrical link between the upper and lower levels of the garden. Other custom-designed features would include a glass-cube screen, a pergola, a state-of-the-art barbecue and a pool bar.

SOLUTION

By craning in twenty-eight mature palm trees, all of the same height, Randle not only provided instant structure but screened off the garden from adjacent houses. The foliage of the palm trees is level with the upper windows of the house next door. Western red cedar trellising was installed between the clients' property and the adjacent one; within two years, this was festooned by white bougainvillea, making an attractive boundary.

Further privacy was provided by a spectacular curtain of water made to Randle's own design, a 4 x 2 metre/13 x 7 foot structure of woven stainless-steel mesh, down which water continually shimmers. Not only is this an effective screening feature, but it makes an eye-catching focal point for those entering the house. Further interest has been created through custom-made columns of glass cubes, which rotate

on stainless-steel poles, catching the sun during the day and artificially lit by night.

The rows of steps from the terrace down to the pool are made to two heights: shallow ones for walking down, and treble-height ones that create an interesting visual division between the upper and lower levels. Here Randle designed another water feature: a limestone basin of water, which brims over, sending a weir down the central steps. Stepping stones separate the main pool from a hydrotherapy area, where the measurements of the clients' bodies provided a blueprint for contours within the pool's structure; this means they can sit in perfect comfort while enjoying a jacuzzi massage.

The main terrace includes a custom-built barbecue and a bar, while to the front of the house is a secluded terrace and pergola, ideal for enjoying the morning sun. Durable Dedon

ABOVE LEFT AND RIGHT: The garden under construction. At this stage, the palm trees Randle introduced are the only planting in evidence.

ABOVE: With the palm trees *in situ*, the rest of the garden begins to take shape. Dedon furniture has been chosen to reflect the modernist architecture. The adjoining pool with integral, contoured water beds was designed by Randle.

woven furniture complements the ultra-contemporary style and can also withstand high temperatures. French limestone was chosen for use throughout – this too is ideal in a warm climate.

Lighting is also an important feature of the scheme. There are recessed downlighters integrated into the front wall, fibreoptics for the water features, and uplighters recessed into the paving on the terrace to light the glass cubes.

PLANTING

Three mature olive trees to the front and the twenty-eight mature palm trees to the rear provide the core of the planting. A hedge of architectural cypress trees has also been introduced to emphasize the structure. The client specified a planting scheme of aromatic blues and whites, so Randle created a palette of jasmines, plumbago, white 'Iceberg' roses, lavender, agapanthus, frangipani, aquilegia and locally sourced bougainvillea.

'If you opt for limestone, make sure you choose a variety suited to the temperature in your garden and seal the underside if necessary. Here we used white cement and whitewashed sand for the grouting. If you make the wrong choices, you will end up ripping it all out and starting again – a costly and time-wasting exercise.'

RESULT

The garden took about two years to complete because of building licence issues, although the planting itself took only an astonishing six days, excluding the palm trees. The clients are delighted with the result, a truly holistic design that was tailor-made to fulfil all their requirements and which they say exceeded their most optimistic expectations.

ABOVE: Columns of glass cubes, designed by Randle, rotate in the *al fresco* dining area, catching the light by day and night.
TOP RIGHT: In the hot climate, meals are eaten outside and often cooked in this high-tech barbecue kitchen area.
FAR RIGHT: A recessed line of LEDs lights the cascading water feature, which is constructed of fine woven stainless-steel mesh, giving the water a shimmery effect.
RIGHT: This shallow limestone basin provides another water feature on the terrace, sending water cascading down to the pool below.

THE REMODELLED GARDEN

Some of my clients are fortunate enough to live in houses that are historically significant, with gardens that have a long provenance and which need particular understanding and care. It is not necessarily a question of restoring a garden to the exact design of many hundreds of years ago – gardens are not meant to be museums – but certainly a designer needs to have a respect for the past and for the previous great landscape architects who once left their signature on the land.

'Capability' Brown is probably one of the best-known landscape designers in history. The first case study I have included here once benefited from the great man's touch. By the time I became involved, all trace of his work had long disappeared, but even so it was essential to accurately pinpoint where his original gardens had stood, in order not to disturb any trace of them that might still lie under the soil. It was inspiring and humbling to think that he had once surveyed the same ground and brought his vision to that house and location. I hope he would have approved of how it looks today.

The second is a garden built on the site of ancient parkland, once the backdrop to a country mansion. It is an example of how to balance twenty-first-century architecture with existing specimen trees and period features. The third is a garden built on the site of a much older one: here it was a case of creating a new design that would appear to have bedded down over time and be in complete sympathy with the period property. The fourth is, unusually, a hotel in Syria, once a family's ancient palatial home with an existing series of courtyard gardens that needed to be rejuvenated while losing none of their traditional charm or character. In each case, my aim was to find a connection with the past and an understanding of the original vision, but then to reinterpret the design for a whole new generation. Gardens have to move on, but that isn't to say they should lose their historic roots.

Randle designed a series of courtyard gardens for the Beit Salahieh Hotel in Aleppo, Syria.

'We have given the house a soul outside that it already had inside. When I first saw the house, I drove through a cold open void from gate to door. Now the garden is singing and dancing.'

ABOVE: A detail of the wrought-iron gates that lead to this Grade I-listed house.
RIGHT: A view of the house from the far side of the river, along which mature specimen trees thrive.
OPPOSITE ABOVE: One of the first things Randle did was recreate the drive. He constructed the new one from granite setts, giving a sense of arrival through the mature avenue leading to the house.
OPPOSITE BELOW: The parterre gardens that lead from the house feature a series of magnificent urns that have been copied from an antique Italian design.

HISTORY & PROVENANCE

This Grade I-listed house was for many years the headquarters of an international company, and by the time these clients bought it as a private residence, it had acquired a very institutional air. Randle was introduced to the project by the interior designer Alex Kravetz. Although the grounds were Grade II listed, at first glance they did not seem to have much of merit. In fact there has been a garden here since Tudor times and in the eighteenth century Capability Brown landscaped a section of the estate. There are some spectacular trees, including London planes, but essentially it was one big open space devoid of interest. Its most picturesque feature was the river that meanders through it, overhung with trees.

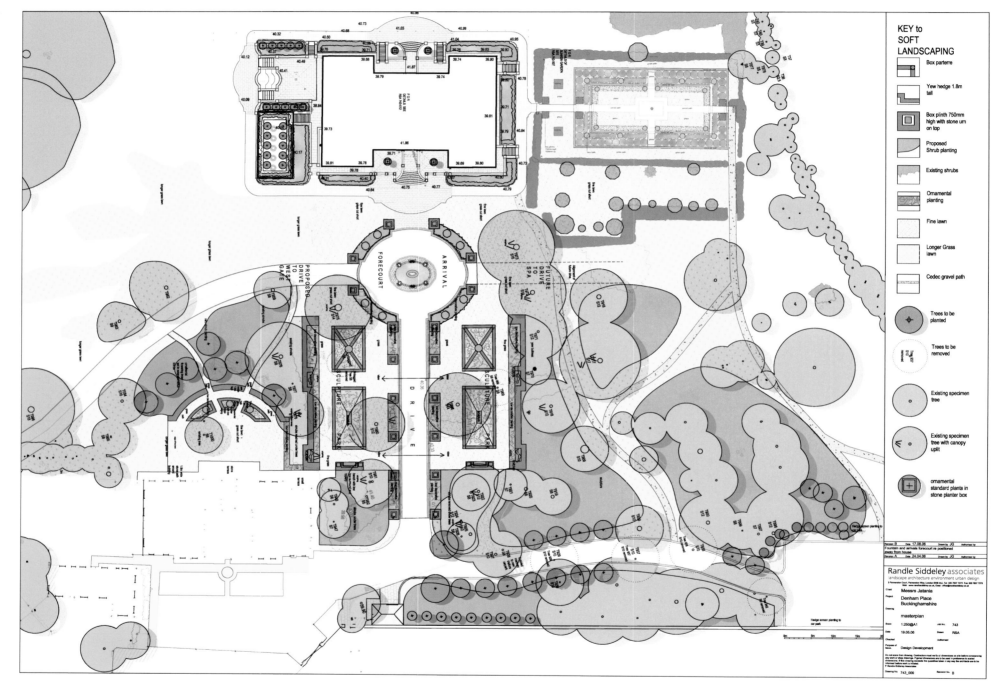

LEFT: Randle's master plan for the garden shows the complexity of merging new garden areas into the existing landscape.
ABOVE: A yew crescent screens the Georgian clock house from the main house and creates the perfect backdrop for a series of parterres.

VISION

This is an outstanding house, but over the years the setting had become tired and unloved. Randle wanted to restore the grounds to their original importance and beauty. It was essential to create the right first impression, and then to restore the series of gardens immediately around the house, so that they would complement both each other and the history of the building.

CHALLENGES

The first step was to undertake a full historic survey. The Capability Brown landscape had long been lost, but it was important to know exactly where his design lay, so as not to disturb what remained.

An unprepossessing driveway of ubiquitous tarmac and bricks led from the main gates to the house, giving no sense of the provenance and importance of the architecture. Randle wanted to relocate the drive to follow the original one, now

reduced to a bumpy grass track, which crossed the river over an ornate stone bridge. However, this route gave a view to a Georgian clock house, which clashed architecturally with the main house and so was in need of screening.

There was also a great deal of essential maintenance to carry out, including the clearing of woodland and the de-silting of the river. Lawn areas had to be restored through a careful programme of scarifying, overseeding and topdressing. It was also necessary to protect the garden from the deer that wander wild in this area.

SOLUTION

The original driveway has now been fully restored with granite setts laid the whole length. Its route allows visitors to appreciate the full beauty of the property as they approach – a sensational view of splendid tree specimens, the river and then the house itself. An avenue of parterre gardens punctuated by handsome urns – copied from one original – leads to the main door, giving a sense of grandeur and anticipation. These parterres have been sympathetically placed around existing lime trees.

ABOVE: The restored sunken garden, framed with yew hedging, features a deep yew alcove sheltering a classical statue and is surrounded by perennial planting. RIGHT: The parterre garden that leads to the house has been skilfully planned around the existing avenue of lime trees.

'With a house as magnificent as this one, it is important to have year-round interest and structure. I wanted the owners to enjoy vistas to their garden from every part of the house at all times of the year. The urns that line the drive are one example of this, providing as they do a backbone to the design. Yew and box hedging also defines different sections of the landscape, its crisp and clear lines contrasting beautifully with the softer planting.'

Usefully, the de-silting of the river provided rich topsoil for these gardens.

A yew crescent has been planted around the clock house, providing a screen from the drive and giving the building its own private garden area. The grounds immediately around the house were also in need of long-overdue attention. These include a spectacular sunken garden with clipped box features and a yew alcove. Now replanted, this looks particularly glorious through the summer months. Adjacent to it is the champagne garden, named after the topiary Irish yews, which resemble champagne flutes. The original layout has been kept, but the yews were in need of skilful pruning to restore them to their former glory.

PLANTING

The planting scheme was designed to give particular richness and colour from spring through to the end of summer. Extensive use of box hedging along the drive creates a frame for spring bulbs and herbaceous perennials, including oriental poppies, cynara, cardoons, anemones, penstemons, ornamental alliums, lilies and tulips. Standard roses include three pink varieties: 'Albertine', 'Super Fairy' and 'Gertrude Jekyll'. Shrubs such as ligustrum, lavender, hebe and salvia, slightly less formal in structure, provide a contrast with the clipped box.

RESULT

Although the garden is not yet finished – there are plans to tackle the old walled garden next – this is a landscape that has been totally transformed over the last seven years. The clients are delighted: Randle's design is a wonderful achievement and one of the highlights of the house's history so far.

SYMPATHY & HARMONY

ABOVE: John Brown's *Family at Play* sculpture is a delightful focal point on the lawn.
ABOVE RIGHT: The area around the eighteenth-century orangery has been sympathetically planted with Italian pencil cypress trees to accentuate the structure.

These clients approached Randle when they commissioned Munkenbeck & Marshall to build them a new house on the site of the Grade II-listed Stanmore Park estate in north London. He was appointed to advise on the landscape planning, design and construction for this award-winning new build. The garden is about 1.6 hectares/4 acres, half of which are woodland – mainly beech, ash and silver birch. The curtilage includes the old orangery that once formed part of the estate and some ancient, protected cedar, yew and oak trees. There were a natural brook running through the grounds and an eighteenth-century grotto to the front of the property, in need of repair.

The house is constructed of natural materials, including stone walling, exposed brick and western red cedar. The design also features an 'indoor-outdoor' swimming pool.

ABOVE: Ornamental grasses look
pleasing against the new house
and moated extension.

'This is a project that is all about integrating the past
with the present. It was important that the garden
design be strong enough to stand up to the Munkenbeck
& Marshall architecture; that landscape and building
worked together successfully. I wanted to feel that the
garden came right up to these wonderful, huge windows,
so directly against the building I used ornamental
grasses, which filter the light and lead the eye to
the trees and sky beyond.'

CHALLENGE

The site was completely overgrown with stinging nettles,
brambles and other invasive weeds. One unexpected
feature is that although the garden is located on one of the
highest points in the vicinity, the water table is only about 30
centimetres/12 inches below the surface. This created huge
drainage problems. The clients' first request was for Randle's
team to demolish the house they were replacing. This
provided a huge pile of rubble that was kept on site for use
as hardcore. The woodland area needed clearing where trees
had collapsed, so those were chipped and again kept on site.
The biggest challenge was the lack of usable topsoil once the
new house was constructed – the use of heavy machinery on a
site such as this damages the structure of soil permanently.

VISION

Randle wanted to balance the new garden with the existing
grounds, including the cedar trees and woodland. He also

LEFT ABOVE: The wall is an extension of the wall of the house. The slot allows an enticing view from one aspect to another.
LEFT BELOW: Pencil cypress trees around the orangery are complemented by a parterre of box, lavender and day lilies.
ABOVE: Looking through the slot in the wall you can see the orangery – a glimpse back in time.

wanted to create a powerful effect by using water to reflect trees and sky. He envisaged a contemporary 'moat' of interconnecting pools, balanced by the indoor-outdoor swimming pool at the other end of the building. He also recognized that the planting design should be relatively simple: a terrace area framed by a sea of tall grasses to add texture and movement to the landscape. Boundaries were to be planted with yew, hollies, willows and pines, all within a framework of indigenous hedges. The stream that runs through the garden would be transformed into romantic garden space.

SOLUTION

The ground had been so destabilized by the time the new house was complete, and the water table was so naturally high, that it was imperative a land drainage system be introduced. This was designed to hold a certain amount of water, so that now the clients' children can run around

on the grass and play football rather than sinking in their wellies. So much of the topsoil had lost structure because of the rigours of the building works that tons of lorry loads had to be removed and then replaced with the same amount of new topsoil. That was one of the biggest costs of the garden and a frustrating one, as there was nothing to see for such a sizeable outlay of money.

The house design utilized a lot of natural stone and exposed brick, so hard surfaces in the garden were chosen to complement these. A thick band of grey limestone was chosen to border the house and continue around the pool. Randle turned a redundant car parking space, where water naturally collected, into a shallow pond with a timber bridge across it, linking the children's tree house – built in one of the ancient cedar trees – to the main garden.

PLANTING

The surround of the house has been planted with multi-stemmed river birch trees and ornamental grasses, such as miscanthus, *Stipa gigantea* and calamagrostis. The latter are particularly eye-catching when juxtaposed with contemporary architecture: they are like a fringe that frames the face of the building, softening the structure of walls and paving. Tall Italian cypress trees are planted around the orangery to frame the building and add structural interest. A small parterre garden of box, herbs and cutting flowers

ABOVE: The indoor-outdoor swimming-pool is bordered with ornamental grasses, echoing the natural landscape beyond.
RIGHT: Pools of water around the house are a contemporary equivalent of the moat and add another layer of reflection, interest and beauty.
FAR RIGHT: The children's play area features a wonderful tree house, constructed around an ancient cedar tree.

'It is fun to add witty and unexpected touches within the design of a garden that give visitors pleasure when they happen upon them. Here Munkenbeck & Marshall had closed off the view to the garden from the front of the house by continuing an indoor wall outside the house for a further 5 metres/16 feet, so dovetailing it into the landscape. However, we had the idea of cutting a slot into this, giving a hint of the landscape beyond. On the other side of the wall, out of sight, I added a water feature: a weir of water that cascades from a stainless-steel lip and is then carried to reflective pools that lie beyond the smoking room and library. Visitors turn a corner and come across this spectacular fall of water.'

has also been planted here, in keeping with the orangery's historic architecture; a wildflower meadow has been created to the right of this for contrast. The stream garden features shade-tolerant tree ferns, hostas, camellias, primulas, ferns and azaleas, which complement the indigenous trees and shrubs. In the main garden, perennials give colour and shape throughout the summer months: species include helenium, agapanthus, verbena, hosta, heuchera, primula and iris.

RESULT

The whole family love the garden and make good use of it. The children have plenty of space for outdoor games and a fantastic tree house. Importantly, the garden is in complete harmony with the spirit and style of the architecture. The chosen artwork also reflects this, notably John Brown's *Family at Play* sculpture.

WAKING A SLEEPING BEAUTY

'This is a garden on a very grand scale, so it took many years to implement the designs in full. It was not just a case of renovating the gardens themselves, but of making sure the totality worked – parkland, lake, farm buildings and all. The proof of its success lies in there always being heart-stopping views wherever in the garden you happen to stand'

This country estate is on the site of a much older one. The original Georgian house was demolished in the 1960s, but the new owners commissioned Sir William Whitfield to rebuild in the same Palladian style on the existing footprint. The house is now regarded as the finest classical country house built in Britain for seventy years or more. The structure of the original formal gardens, created in the 1930s, had survived but was greatly in need of renovation. The gardens are substantial – about 4 hectares/10 acres, not including the surrounding acres of parkland, which date from the eighteenth century.

LEFT: Verdant herbaceous borders provide a focal point to the garden in summer months and are contrasted here with clipped balls of ligustrum on the terrace above.
ABOVE: The sunken garden prior to renovation.

CHALLENGE

The design of the new house was conceived in harmony with the restoration of the park. The historic layout included a rectangular canal, the Long Water, and radiating avenues of lime trees. The design also needed to include a series of formal gardens, including parterres, that would reflect the provenance of the house. In addition, it was desirable to re-route the driveway so that the house was approached via open parkland, rather than past unsightly farm buildings.

The sunken garden had to include habitat for the protected great crested newts that live there.

VISION

Randle was one of the designers involved with the rejuvenation of the gardens over a period of fifteen years. He planned the renovation of formal areas, such as the sunken garden, clipped yews and herbaceous borders, which was also to include the remodelling of the Long Water. This

would now be made to sweep around the rear of the house, to create an inspiring vista.

SOLUTION

The relocation of the driveway and the restoration of the lake were both intensely complicated projects, but once completed they gave the house the grand setting it deserved. A new gatehouse was built, adjacent to the main road. From here, the drive leads over open parkland to where the full splendour of the house is revealed. Additional ponds and lakes were renovated; thousands of trees planted in the parkland; and a pedimented temple built,

the latter providing a striking view across the lake. Stone-paved terraces with long rectangular ponds – a feature of the original garden – have been revived, and the grounds around the house restored to their 1930s glory. These include the formal sunken garden with central pond.

PLANTING

On the terraces, pyramids of clipped yew lead the eye across rectangular ponds to the grass terraces beyond. The surrounding landscape is relatively flat, so height is suggested through standard trees of box positioned on top of the terrace walls. Deep herbaceous borders use abundant

ABOVE: A view of the remodelled sunken garden during the first stage of planting. Architectural elements, such as box and cypress, have now been added.
RIGHT ABOVE: White has been used to great effect in the sunken garden, including the English roses 'Winchester Cathedral' and 'Glamis Castle'.
RIGHT BELOW: The sunken garden in full flower today. The herbaceous perennials here include delphinium, salvia, aquilegia, alchemilla and verbena.

'It may be that you want to rejuvenate your garden but cannot afford to do everything at once. The best investment is a master plan created by the designer of your choice – a blueprint that can be initiated in stages. Once you have agreed on the total vision for the garden, it is much easier to decide where the priorities are. You can then budget accordingly. It may take a few years to do everything you would like, but it is unlikely you will have to wait for fifteen!'

combinations of peonies, roses, lavender, hostas, geraniums, clematis, hydrangeas, irises, scabious, sedums, euphorbia and alchemilla, creating a symphony of colour – mainly in gentle tones of pink, white and soft blue. The sunken garden is framed with box hedging, punctuated by pencil-like cypress trees. Here herbaceous borders have a strong white, blue and violet theme, including *Anemone* 'Whirlwind', *Delphinium* 'Casablanca', *Salvia* 'May Night', *Iris* 'Jane Philips', *Alchemilla mollis*, verbena, aquilegia and 'Winchester Cathedral' roses.

RESULT

This is a landscape that looks as though it has been unchanged for centuries, which is exactly what Randle wanted to achieve. The garden may be large, but it is broken down into a series of individual 'rooms' that each offers pleasing vistas from one to the other. The design also allows for magnificent, open views to the parkland and countryside beyond.

ARABIAN TREASURE

'It was a huge compliment to be asked to work on such a prestigious project in the old city. In many ways, it was a huge learning curve for all the team – different culture, different climate, different skills base available – but to see the results now is truly heartlifting. It was not just our expertise that went into its creation, but that of the project leader Adli Qudsi, architect Thierry Grandin, interior designers Anne Judet and Catherine Chasset, and Andrew Moore, the specialist in glass who took my concept for the water feature and made it reality.'

ABOVE: One of the internal courtyard gardens Randle remodelled, being careful to plant indigenous species in order to retain the original character. OPPOSITE: At night, the gardens are lit to magical effect; illuminated water is particularly atmospheric.

Aleppo is poised to become one of the most chic destinations in the Middle East. The largest city in Syria, it was historically significant as the end of the Silk Road, a strategic position that once attracted traders from as far afield as China to the east and Europe to the west. To this day it is home to the largest *suq* (covered market) in the world, including the famous Medina. The medieval architecture of the old enclosed city has been well preserved and in recent years has undergone a wave of successful restorations. The huge medieval castle – the Citadel of Aleppo – is one of the oldest and largest in the world, meticulously restored in recent years with help from the Aga Khan Trust for Culture.

Randle was approached by a client he has known for many years to help in the transformation of one of the city's historic palaces, now a hotel. The Beit Salahieh is owned by husband-and-wife team Hana and Faisal Al-Kudsi, and was for generations one of the family homes. Now, after painstaking restoration, it is set to become one of Aleppo's growing collection of five-star luxury hotels. Randle's brief was to rejuvenate a series of existing courtyard gardens – the heart of the building – as well as designing a newly created garden to the rear of the building and redesigning the roof terrace on the third floor.

CHALLENGE

The palace is now restored to its former medieval glory, but it was important also to project a flavour of contemporary luxury living in order to attract the sophisticated international clients that it aims to please. Randle set out to create a piece of theatre on the roof terrace by designing a striking bespoke water sculpture made of enormous sheets of backlit glass. The local workforce – highly skilled in many ways – had no experience of making such a technically demanding piece

of sculpture, so it had to be created and shipped from the UK and then craned into place. With the material being glass, none of this was straightforward. As the venture was commercial, it was also of particular importance to work within budget and time constraints.

VISION

Randle took his inspiration from the hotel's spectacular location, with magnificent views from the roof terrace

ABOVE: The bar of the roof terrace is separated from the dining area by a wall of water, which is lit at night with four revolving colours to create atmosphere. This is one of Randle's bespoke designs.
RIGHT: The water feature, seen from the dining side of the terrace. Specially designed canopies offer protection from the sun.

to the citadel. He also conducted extensive research to ensure that the gardens he created were in the spirit of those that would have been here hundreds of years ago. It was important to him that there was a sense of timelessness, given the historic location, but that the design was also imbued with a sense of modernity.

SOLUTION

Randle wanted each of the traditional courtyard gardens to have its own unique character. In redesigning them he used plants grown locally to order: an olive tree terrace in one area; a single dominant palm in another; a plunge pool surrounded by jasmine, damask roses and citrus trees in a third.

On the roof terrace, he designed canopies that are stretched across specially installed columns, so that it is possible to sit and enjoy the view by day without discomfort.

Custom-designed banquette seating, piled with cushions, lines the perimeter. An ultra-chic bar sits centre stage, and from here guests can look through the magnificent wall of water to the citadel beyond.

He also made good use of the incredible skill of the local stone-cutters, restoring existing stone floors and designing new ones in the traditional style.

PLANTING

Plants were chosen that were able to withstand both the high summer temperatures and the very cold winters, as well as for fragrance, form and colour. On the lower floors, lush green planting provides a strong palette, such as *Pittosporum tobira* 'Nanum' and mundo grass (*Ophiopogon japonicus*), complemented by swathes of gardenias and roses. On the roof terrace, three specimens of semi-mature *Lagerstroemia indica*, with exotic flowers, make a striking

focal point. Surrounding planters contain a mix of species such as lavender, agapanthus and rhaphiolepsis.

RESULT

Guests of the Beit Salahieh will not be disappointed. Step out of the lift on to the roof terrace and the heart skips a beat. The water feature is a triumphant addition to the magnificence of the location, and a symbol of Aleppo's changing fortunes. Each of the individual courtyard gardens is spectacular in its different way, a perfectly balanced bridge between the old and the new.

The rooftop restaurant with its magnificent views to the citadel of Aleppo. Stone planters feature lagerstroemia, *Jasminum sambac*, fragrant climbing roses under-planted by Mansouriya roses and various aromatics.

'Syria has fantastic quantities of local limestone available, and the craft skills to make good use of it. Generally speaking, you should use indigenous varieties of stone in your own garden as far as possible – not least because of the environmental impact of shipping it around the world in large quantities. When choosing stone and timber, you also have to take climate into consideration. Here pale stone was chosen because it would reflect light rather than absorb it. Western red cedar was also used, because it is tough enough to withstand the high temperatures.'

THE REJUVENATED GARDEN

In many of the gardens I undertake, the biggest challenge is to persuade the clients that it is worth taking a whole new approach to the outdoor space that they have got used to over time. So many gardens are far from realizing their true potential, because – excuse the pun – people just can't see the wood for the trees. Re-landscaping an existing garden can be just as costly and labour intensive as starting from a blank canvas, so understandably people often baulk at the cost. However, the fact is that a beautiful garden is such an asset to a property that it is always money well spent. Not only that, but once the transformation is complete many people fall in love with their homes all over again and forget all plans of moving.

Here I have chosen two examples of a radical revamp. The first is a London home that had been lived in by the same family for many years, but which had become very 'stuck'. A radical facelift was called for to give it new vigour and life. The second is a suburban garden built around an attractive period house, which was completely lacking in interest. It had no harmony with the architecture and style of the building whatsoever, and so was in desperate need of a fresh eye. I like to think that both gardens have undergone a transformation that will stand them in good stead for many years to come.

Grass steps edged with old York stone were created to make an attractive new entrance, harmonizing the old with the new in this English country garden.

A GARDEN FACELIFT

'This is one of my personal favourites of all the gardens we have designed because we took something that was very tired and turned it into an absolute gem. I went there to dinner after it was finished and thought: "This really could not be any better."'

RIGHT: This dining area has been set into the intersection of a pergola walkway, featuring classical stone columns.
OPPOSITE: A stepping-stone path, edged with box, lavender, santolina, salvia and anthemis, leads from the house to this ornamental gazebo.

After twenty-seven years of one family's use, this large garden in Hampstead, London, was in need of a radical rethink. A fresh eye was needed to breathe new life and character into its design.

GARDEN PLAN 1:50

CHALLENGE

Many years previously, the clients had installed a kidney-shaped swimming pool, which their children had enjoyed when growing up. Now, however, it was barely used at all. If the garden were to take on new shape and stature, the pool would have to go. The clients were persuaded to replace it with a less dominant hot tub.

VISION

Randle wanted to inject the garden with both classical and country references. He planned a path to lead all round the garden, to include a stone-columned pergola leading to a dining terrace. The focal point would be a pretty, octagonal gazebo with tile-pitched roof. The effect would be magical and romantic.

SOLUTION

Removing the pool was the first step, but this was by no means simple. The soil in this area is predominantly clay, so removing something as solidly built as a reinforced steel pool would probably result in subsidence. It took two weeks to reduce the pool by 1 metre – enough to bury it – and then holes were drilled into its base to prevent it from rising to the surface again. All the hardcore was buried in the pool, again to minimize the possibility of it moving.

Tall conifers around the property were left *in situ*, as they

ABOVE: Randle's design for the garden shows the clear delineation between formal paved walkways and terraces and less formal lawned areas.
OPPOSITE: An ornamental stone urn set in a stone circle makes an eye-catching centrepiece at the front of the house.

'Front gardens are like hallways: they create the first impression for any visitor. In a house of distinction, like this one, it is important to set a tone that suits the architecture and period of the property. Although I was mainly concerned with transforming the rear garden, I put aside some of the budget to make sure that the front garden was improved. Now the drive drops down from the main road to a semicircular driveway, surrounded by trees and greenery. A handsome stone urn makes a pleasing feature to greet visitors on arrival.'

created a screen from neighbouring houses. Everything else from the existing garden was stripped out, so that the new design could be implemented. A D-shaped terrace of French limestone trimmed with York stone was built out from the main house, which included a dining area. To the left of this a pergola walkway leads around the lawn along one boundary of the garden and turns the corner along the next. A second dining terrace is set into this bend. The pergola walkway continues to the gazebo, which can also be accessed via grass-set stepping stones from the main terrace. Beyond the gazebo is a second lawned area, its boundaries planted with shrubs and flowers that thrive in the acid soil. Mature specimens were used to create an instant effect.

PLANTING

Most of the planting is evergreen or perennial, with seasonal and highly scented planting reserved for pots, troughs and beds close to the house. The acid soil is perfect for rhododendrons, camellias and magnolias. The path leading to the gazebo is edged with an aromatic mix of lavender, salvia, santolina and anthemis, interspersed with box balls. Wisteria and climbing roses have been trained up the pergola that frames the dining area. Traditional favourites such as delphiniums, roses, lavender and anemones make a summery display at the front of the house.

RESULT

Today this has the reputation of being one of the most wonderful gardens in the area. The clients had been on the verge of putting the house up for sale, but they were so happy with the garden that they decided to stay. And they never did install that hot tub!

SOMETHING OLD, SOMETHING NEW

'The problem of how to integrate new-build areas with original architecture is a common one. The best thing is to use as much greenery as possible – architectural trees, prolific climbers, turf borders and rich planting – to distract the eye from harsh lines and building materials that have not yet had a chance to "weather in". '

LEFT: Creamy yellow York stone was chosen for the terraced areas, here complemented by olive trees, white agapanthus and lavender, which give a contrasting effect during the summer.
RIGHT: The architecture of the house has been softened by planting, including cypress trees and wisteria.

This house was the home of some American clients who had settled in England for a couple of years. The interior designer Joanna Wood introduced Randle to them. The sloping garden had a beautiful avenue of rhododendrons at its centre but was lacking in year-round interest. Situated in the heart of Berkshire, it led down to a golf course and was surrounded by green spaces, but the design did not appear to link well with its surroundings.

LEFT: Where old meets new: a fan of stone steps helps minimize the effect of the over-bold design of the swimming-pool extension, built by a previous developer.
RIGHT: The colonnades of the original house have been planted with wisteria, which will grace the walls, too, once mature.

CHALLENGE

A swimming-pool wing had been built on to the main house, and it was unsympathetic in style to the rest of the architecture. From this extension, very steep and unsafe steps led down to an unsightly water feature with a boulder as its dominant focal point. This area was in need of a major redesign. The rest of the garden needed to be brought up to a better standard of design, so that it did not appear to be the poor relation to the house itself. As the clients knew they would not be staying very long, this had to be achieved within a relatively modest budget.

VISION

As well as integrating the new extension with the original architecture, Randle wanted to find new ways of opening up the garden and linking it to the countryside around. His aim was to give the garden immediately around the house a summery Mediterranean ambience. He also wanted to

modernize the rest of the garden, including the driveway, which was very tired.

SOLUTION

The original terrace was rebuilt, using a creamy yellow York stone, and pushed out about 3 metres/10 feet deep, so improving access to the garden views. A double flight of sawn York stone steps framed by Italian cypress now leads to the garden. Randle also planted a line of pleached lime trees to soften the ugly elevation of the swimming-pool extension. As these have matured, they have created a thick band of green that breaks up the solid mass of brick and roof.

The steep, uneven steps from the extension have been replaced by an elegant fan of wide York stone ones. These in turn lead to a flight of turf steps with stone treads, leading down to the lower garden. The change from stone to grass signifies the transition from the formality of the building to the informality of this part of the garden.

PLANTING

Opposite the colonnade of the main terrace is a Mediterranean border of olive trees, complemented by lavender and white agapanthus. At the far end of the terrace is the line of pleached lime trees. These create a pleasing contrast with the deep greenery of the rhododendrons, as well as disguising the extension. Adjacent herbaceous borders are filled with a rich mix of alliums, salvia and irises. The surround of the house has been softened using Italian cypress trees, wisteria and a number of olive trees underplanted with lavender.

RESULT

The clients were persuaded to spend more money than they had originally budgeted for, but were well rewarded financially when they sold up to return to the USA a few years later. The redesign gave them a generous-sized terrace for entertaining, new vistas to the surrounding countryside, a more balanced garden layout and harmony between the opposing architectural styles of the building. A new driveway was also laid, making the perfect place for their children to skateboard.

'We use carefully drawn perspectives to show clients what they should expect once we have finished. This is essential in a project like this, where it is quite hard for an untrained eye to imagine existing architecture transformed into something much more harmonious. Once the clients saw the visuals and understood what we needed to do, they were happy to bring in specialists.'

STYLE

Style is such a huge word it can be overwhelming and even alienating. But if you are to design a garden successfully, you need to understand where your personal style lies. Do you favour complicated tapestries of planting or simple, clean schemes? Are you a traditionalist or a minimalist? An urbanite or a country soul? It is possible to mix traditional with contemporary, just as you would in the home, but it has to be done with sensitivity and restraint.

When I first make a site visit to clients, I don't just look at the garden. I look at the architecture of the house, the interior design, how they dress – clues, in other words, to where their aesthetic sense lies. It is enormously helpful if they have also taken the trouble to collect tear sheets from magazines or marked pages within books that show the sorts of gardens they like. Sometimes one picture can tell me everything I need to know about the direction they want to go in and how it might be reinterpreted for their own outdoor space. I never design a garden that is the same as another, as this book illustrates, because every person I design for is different and no two locations are ever the same. Each garden is created with certain people and a certain location in mind, whether contemporary or classic, formal or fun. The important thing is to find a style that allows the owner's own taste and personality to find expression.

The fact is that style gives a signature to a garden that affects every choice, from paving stones and summer houses to furniture and flowers. There should be a sense of cohesion running through the design, just as you have in the best-designed houses. It is not that everything has to look blandly the same, but just as inside a house it would be jarring and confusing to walk from room to room and feel as if each is fighting with the others, so it is in the garden: you can introduce different styles in outdoor 'rooms', but linking them should be one master vision.

BOUNDARIES

The boundaries are of course akin to the dividing walls within a house. Which type of material you choose to denote boundaries has an impact on the whole look of a garden. In cities, there is a natural tendency to opt for high, solid boundaries, such as brick walls, because of privacy issues. However, you may do better to lower them slightly and enjoy borrowed views over neighbouring gardens. Neighbours are entitled to 'rights of light' in any case, so although you can increase a boundary height with open trellis, there is a limit as to how high walls or solid fences can be built.

Remember that hard surfaces, such as walls and trellis, take a while to weather in and will look totally transformed once they are covered with climbers or hung with pots. Painting them can also soften their effect. Hedges are an attractive alternative, but don't let them grow too high – lines of towering leylandii are the curse of the suburbs.

In rural gardens, hedges are the natural choice, as they merge with the landscape beyond. You could choose evergreens, such as yew, or species such as beech that will brown and thin in the winter season. This isn't necessarily a bad thing: they will become part of the character of the winter garden.

Of course you may also need boundaries of one form or other within the garden, to screen off different sections, such as a vegetable garden or children's play area. Again you should consider all the possible options. For example, you might want a wall around a swimming pool to protect you from wind, but perhaps you could cut an opening so that the view beyond can still be enjoyed, or plant a windbreak of trees instead. A pergola walkway is also an attractive way of linking two sections of the garden, while screening one from the other.

HARD SURFACES

Stone is the flooring of the garden. More than any other ingredient, it dominates the style of the overall scheme. It is also one of the most expensive ingredients, so it is essential to make the right choice. This is where the eye and experience of a professional designer come into play. There are so many varieties of colour, texture, type and size of stone available that it can be bewildering. Limestone has been popular in recent years, particularly in city gardens, but traditional York stone also has its devotees. You may want to mix two types of stone for contrasting effect, perhaps introducing a chequerboard pattern. This can be particularly effective in a smart city garden (see page 129). The important thing is to do your research and gather samples of paving that you can study outside in all types of weather. Remember there are maintenance issues with your choice, too. Overhanging trees will stain pale limestone, for example, so you must make sure it is possible to keep it clean at all times. There are also safety aspects to consider, particularly in swimming-pool areas, where you need stone that has non-slip properties.

The type of stone that you choose for the paving should also be used on adjacent structures such as steps, retaining walls, terrace boundaries and suchlike. All that stone can seem overwhelming when you first see it *in situ*, so allow the eye to adjust over a few days; once the garden is planted and in its maturity, the stone will not seem so dominant. Remember that you are using it to create a blank canvas on which the rest of the garden will be created; therefore you need to choose a colour and style that will not fight for your attention once all the other ingredients are in place. Go for neutrality rather than boldness, just as you would if selecting a carpet colour to be used throughout an entire house.

Gravel too comes in a huge array of types, shapes, sizes and colours. A surface such as marble chippings is an excellent alternative to grass in a garden where maintaining a perfect lawn would be difficult (see page 163). A mix of stone paving and gravel works very well: solid paving denotes more formal areas, while stepping stones or gravel paths give a hint of informality. Remember, though, that gravel demands maintenance if it is not going to become a weedy mess.

Brick is also an attractive hard material to introduce into the garden. Old-fashioned red-brick paths look perfect in country settings, and are particularly harmonious with cottage planting. Keep them free of moss so that they do not become treacherous when wet.

Finally, use planting to soften the effect of these hard materials. The chequerboard effect mentioned earlier can be particularly effective if stone slabs alternate with squares of camomile or thyme. Allow plants to grow over the edges of paths to take the sharpness from straight edges. And plant ground-cover varieties at the base of retaining walls and at the side of steps to help assimilate them into the garden.

SLOPES

Over the years, I seem to have designed an unusual amount of gardens with slopes. Sometimes these have involved slopes down to the house; others have had slopes from the house down the garden; and some have combined both. The only practical approach is to use earth-diggers and to transform these slopes into a series of flat terraces, with steps leading from each to the next. Each terrace becomes a garden room, adding to the mystery and excitement of the garden as you explore it further and further.

You will also need retaining walls in order to stop the land moving over time. These require professional help from structural engineers, because the consequences of not making them strong enough could be catastrophic.

Of course slopes nearly always mean drainage issues too, with the lowest points likely to be a sea of mud after rain. Land drainage systems can be used to direct and disperse accumulating water, but you have to be prepared to spend money on something you can't actually see and enjoy. However, without suitable drainage you will never get full use of waterlogged land or be able to plant successfully in it.

WATER

I love water in gardens – not just for its look, but for its sound and for how theatrical it looks when lit at night. It has a textural and playful quality that significantly benefits a garden's design. Not only that but water in the garden is eco-friendly, encouraging birds and insects to visit. Many of my clients are lucky enough to have water running through their gardens – be it a lake, river or brook – but for some, I have created huge expanses of water on what was previously dry land. Anything is possible if you have the budget and the machinery to access the water table, but it is crucial that you understand what you are doing. Flooding either your own home or your neighbour's would be an expensive mistake.

For many people, particularly those with city gardens, the solution is to introduce a custom-made contemporary water feature. I have designed these in many different materials from bronze and stainless steel to limestone and marble. The most practical in terms of space are those that stand vertically with water cascading down into a rill of some sort, before the water is recirculated once more. Lighting can be incorporated into the design; both fibreoptics and LEDs are very effective, while being low on energy consumption. Don't hold back on size – even a tiny garden can benefit from the presence of an imposing slab of water. I also love reviving antique water features, such as stone fountains. There is something gloriously romantic about coming across one of these while walking in a garden.

If you have very small children, even a water feature with a rill is a hazard, so it will need to be contained. When it comes to areas such as swimming pools, it is recommended these be independently enclosed with lockable gates.

It is not easy to introduce water to an existing scheme, although it is not impossible to do so. It is best to get the plumbing laid before you begin planting, even if you cannot afford the water sculpture itself for a while. Don't buy a cheap water feature: if it does not work properly, it will be a source of endless frustration, rather than one of infinite pleasure. Make sure you position it in such a way that you have maximum enjoyment of its sight and sound, both from inside the house and within the garden. The water features I install in city gardens are usually positioned against the rear boundary, so that they can be seen and heard from many different places.

ROOF TERRACES

A roof terrace is a welcome replacement for a garden in a city apartment. When it comes to which surface to choose for the floor, you must be practical. First, there could be weight considerations; for this reason, decking is usually preferable to stone. Second, you need to know that water will drain easily from the terrace after rain, so you might have to plan for gulleys and drains. Third, you need something that is easy to maintain.

Even the smallest roof terrace should have room for some kind of outdoor dining. Make sure it is lit properly at night, so that you can extend the hours it is used and enjoy it from both inside and outside. Finally, make sure that any temporary structures, such as parasols and garden planters, are fully secure and will not fly off with a heavy gust of wind, possibly causing injury to someone below. The smaller the area, the more fun it is to cram it with greenery – small sun traps are ideal for Mediterranean plants such as lemon trees and figs, underplanted with herbs. In more exposed areas, species such as amelanchiers in containers work very well. For all-year interest plant ornamental grasses, such as *Calamagrostis x acutiflora* 'Karl Foerster'.

EATING OUT

One of the joys of having a garden is eating *al fresco* with friends and family. It stands to reason, then, that one of the first things to consider is where best to locate a space for relaxing and for eating. This is usually as close to the house as possible, so that you can access the kitchen easily. French doors opening from the kitchen on to the terrace are ideal – if designing a garden from scratch, make the terrace as wide as you can so that you can fit a generous-sized table with enough space around it for people to move easily. As your dining area will probably be on stone or decking, use containers of plants to soften the effect. Herbs are ideal, giving both scent and offering culinary use.

If your garden is big enough, it is good to have one or two other dining or sitting areas – perhaps one close to a pool or children's play area; looking out over a lovely view; or tucked under the shade of a much-loved tree. It may be that you have a more formal entertaining area on the terrace and a much less formal one tucked deep in the garden; you can ring the change of mood with a different style of furniture and cushions, and even hang bunting or paper lanterns. Lighting is essential to the enjoyment of any such space; for more advice on this, see page 204.

For some people, being able to throw a party in the garden is on their list of essentials. If so, think about this from the beginning of the design process. Some of my clients have bespoke marquees made to fit the dimensions of their garden, so that they can hold parties for a hundred or more even if the weather is less than kind (see page 140). Perhaps you need to look ahead to the possibility of hosting a wedding in your garden or a milestone birthday. The success of such areas all comes down to early planning – not just the space needed, but electricity, lighting, types and heights of plants, and suchlike. The sooner you seek professional advice about what you want to achieve, the better.

Finally, do take time out to sit and enjoy your garden. It is all too easy to spend every moment out there tackling the many jobs there are to be done. But time spent simply looking and appreciating is time well spent indeed.

SCULPTURE AND ART

Sculpture in the garden can be a wonderful addition – the bolder, the better. I particularly love abstract pieces in the tradition of Barbara Hepworth and Henry Moore, and I admire contemporary artists who work within landscape, such as Andy Goldsworthy. In a huge country estate, nothing looks more eye-catching than one enormous spectacular work of art on the horizon: it creates a point of reference around which everything else radiates.

While I am not personally a fan of figurative and fussy antique statuary, I love classical urns of momentous scale. In some of the gardens I have designed, we have bought an original and then had it copied to great effect, creating an avenue of urns. If a client has antique pieces, such as lead troughs, we may find a new use for them, such as in a water feature created around them.

Whatever your taste, deciding where best to position sculpture is crucial. Do you want it as a focal point, to be viewed from every area of the garden? Or do you want to place it in a more hidden spot, so that you discover it when you come around a corner? There is no right or wrong – it depends on the experience you want to create. What is important is to make sure that pieces of sculpture do not fight for attention: a replicated urn which creates one body of work has enormous impact, but a line of disparate works by different artists would look confusing. And it is better to buy one really magnificent work than a whole group of mediocre examples.

GAZEBOS AND FURNITURE

Gazebos and summer houses can be attractive focal points within the garden, but the golden rule is that they must sit happily with the style as a whole. To be honest, my heart always sinks if a client announces that he or she has bought such a structure in isolation. The wrong design can be as jarring as an ugly piece of modern furniture in a room full of Chippendale.

When it comes to furniture, the golden rule is to buy the best you can afford. The garden is an outdoor room to the house; why, then, buy badly designed, cheap furniture that you would not want inside the house? Outdoor furniture is expensive because it has to withstand variations of weather over many years, but as with everything, you get what you pay for. Try to avoid tables with a hole in the middle for parasols. A far better solution is to invest in the free-standing arched variety of sun umbrellas that are counterweighted for balance. These can be directed exactly where you want them and won't be sent flying in the wind.

SWIMMING POOLS

If you have bought a garden with a swimming pool, first ask yourself whether you want to keep it. So often people feel an existing pool should stay, but a design dating from twenty or thirty years ago is unlikely to be a real asset to the garden as a whole. And in all honesty, how often will you really use it if you live in northern Europe? There have been occasions when I have persuaded clients to sacrifice an ugly, barely used pool in order to create an outdoor space of real distinction. So far none has regretted it.

Not that I want to sound anti-pools. For many people they really are part of the quality of life and a centre of family fun. However, by far the best solution is to have a pool separated in some way from the main area of the garden. Swimming pools demand a lot of equipment to maintain them correctly, so a pool house is essential, as is a changing/shower area and a space for entertaining. You are not going to want to walk endlessly backwards and forwards between kitchen and pool, so ideally you need somewhere for a barbecue, fridge, tableware and suchlike.

In other words, a swimming-pool complex demands a lot of design thought before installation. Once you take all of these requirements into consideration, you will probably realize that a much larger area is needed than you anticipated.

And then there is the style of pool. My advice is always to keep it classic and go for a simple rectanglular shape. Curves – as in kidney shapes and the like – date all too fast. You also need something big enough to enjoy a swim as opposed to a soak – 14 x 6 metres/46 x 20 feet is acceptable, but bigger is better. The setting you have chosen should also guide you towards the dimensions – you want something that looks generous where you have located it, not mean. If you have children, make sure you have one built that has safe, wide steps and paint a line beyond which youngsters must not cross unless they can swim well. If you have very deep water for diving at one end, signpost this in a clear way. Because safety is vitally important, site the pool well away from play areas and – if possible – lock gates between pool and garden.

There have been huge improvements in the way that swimming pools are constructed today, particularly with the use of liners. These are essential, because ground moves and you do not want a crack to appear in the base of your pool. A well-designed liner moves with it, preventing damage to the structure of the pool. Which colour and style of tile you choose is a personal preference; on the whole I prefer glass mosaic, which reflects the colour of the sky, rather than imposing a deep blue, which can look artificial. Covers are also a necessity to keep water clean; you should buy the best you can rather than rely on the thin plastic variety (see what I have to say about this on page 183).

If you are lucky enough to have a setting for a pool with a wonderful view, an infinity pool is by far the best choice. This allows the expanse of water to merge with the horizon beyond. Don't destroy the effect with too much stone around it. Apart from stone coping stones for safety, my preference is to turf the area around a pool, so that it harmonizes with the rest of the landscape. Don't fret too much about grass clippings and suchlike getting into the water – it is easy enough to scoop them out each day with a net.

'If a client is having a swimming pool built, I advise that they also have an underground tank installed at the same time for storage of rain and waste water. This is a relatively small additional cost to the building works and it makes sense to do it when everything else is being disrupted. Some of my clients have underground reservoirs that are roughly the same length as the pool and half as wide – a significant amount of storage. Water can then be collected from drainpipes and gulleys, channelled to the tank via underground pipes and then recirculated through an irrigation system to keep the garden watered at dry times of the year. For those interested in sustainability for houses, it is worth noting that there are now systems available that convert collected underground water (which is warmer than surface water) into hot water and heating for the home.'

The lawned area around this pool integrates the pool with the surrounding garden as well as providing a place for seating.

COUNTRY

For many people, a country garden is the ultimate dream. If you are fortunate enough to enjoy a rural location, it stands to reason you need to make style decisions in keeping with the surrounding landscape and buildings. The one big difference between country and urban gardens is that in the former you are usually trying to capitalize on views, existing trees and big skies, while in the latter you are often faced with the problem of trying to screen out much of what surrounds you. It also stands to reason, then, that country gardens are usually best suited to a more informal, less rigid look, so that garden and landscape gently bleed into each other. When I design gardens in the country, very often I find that the biggest problem is editing out obstructions to the views beyond, rather than adding in new features.

The three examples of country style I have chosen here are all as different as can be. The first is an archetypal romantic English country house, which was crying out for a setting as graceful as the architecture. It is a testament to the owner's vision of a truly remarkable remodelling of its surroundings. The second is a beautiful home in the south of France with the most breathtaking views imaginable, but which had little else to commend it when the client took it on. The third also enjoys a glorious English setting, but needed a total makeover in order to do justice to both that and the provenance of the house. Now each is a manifestation of the country dream.

In an idyllic English country garden, topiary yews have been juxtaposed with mature deciduous trees for contrasts of texture and scale and to delineate the croquet lawn edge.

A ROMANTIC PURSUIT

LEFT: The Georgian rectory now enjoys a vista of sympathetically designed gardens, specimen trees and a lake.
ABOVE: The re-routed driveway allows visitors to admire the surrounding parkland on their approach to the house.

This Georgian rectory in Hampshire originally had a modest-sized garden with fields beyond, totalling about 4 hectares/10 acres. The client wanted to replace the fields with parkland and a lake, so that the landscape would be more in keeping with the age of the property. However, instead of one lake, he commissioned three, covering about 2.5 hectares/6 acres. The property specialists Savills introduced Randle to the client; the project manager was John Powell. The lakes had already been constructed, but Randle was invited to take on the landscaping needed to harmonize them with the surroundings.

LEFT: Randle 'naturalized' the lakes with sandstone rocks and lush planting, including swathes of ornamental grasses.
ABOVE: The gardens already had many beautiful specimen trees, such as this platanus. Randle planted clipped yew cones for all-year interest.

CHALLENGE

There was a public right of way, protected by law, which followed a route between the house and the proposed tennis court. This could not be removed, but it was important to find a way of giving the client more privacy, which meant that planning regulations had to be carefully negotiated. In the UK, it is necessary to obtain special consent when turning agricultural land into parkland, although such soft landscaping is often regarded more favourably than solid, fixed objects such as swimming pools and tennis courts. The contours of the land surrounding the house sloped down to the side, and this had to be rectified if the property were ever to sit comfortably within its landscape.

STYLE: COUNTRY

'It is not often I am given the opportunity to create landscapes in the tradition of Capability Brown, and it is really exciting and satisfying to see how these expanses of water inject the garden with romance and grace. For those who have the budget for such ambitious schemes, part of the pleasure lies in how quickly the results can be enjoyed.'

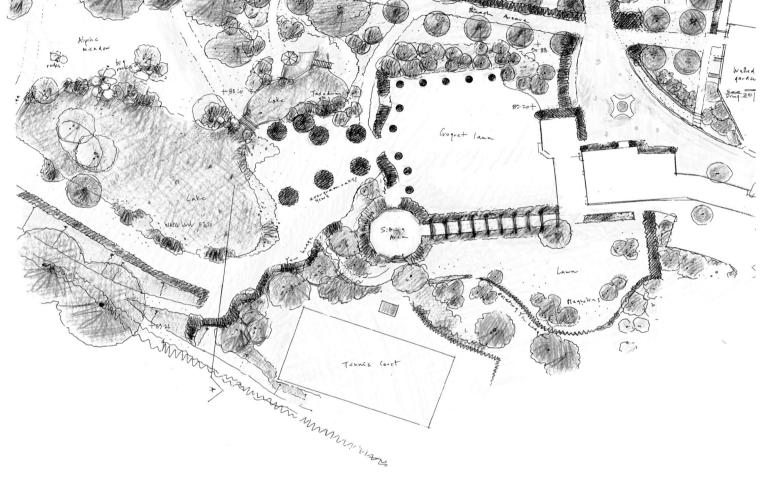

LEFT: This view of the approach to the house in summer shows the harmony between the existing mature trees and the fifty new specimens that were planted.
ABOVE: The original master plan for the property, showing screening for the tennis court and the views down to the lakes.

FOLLOWING PAGES
LEFT: The planting around the lakes, including the splendid *Gunnera manicata* and enormous crocosmia, has now reached maturity and enjoys views of the surrounding landscape.
RIGHT: A summer spectacle: this pergola walkway of 'White Cloud' roses leads to the sunken garden.

VISION

Randle set out to transform completely the character of the property and the way it was approached. Originally, it was accessed via a country lane that led to outbuildings at the rear of the building and then to the main house. Instead, Randle proposed a gracious, sweeping driveway that followed a natural progression through fields, woodland and parkland, passing by the largest lake and then on to the house and gardens beyond. The existing gardens were to be totally re-landscaped, with a croquet lawn and terraces, and the renovation of the original walled garden.

SOLUTION

Since the public right of way could not be removed, Randle decided to disguise it as best as was possible by lowering it out of sight. In order to eradicate the slope of the existing garden, it was necessary to move a large quantity of earth, in effect cutting and filling into the landscape. The excavated earth was then used to create a steep hedged bank on each side of the public footpath, screening off views of the house and tennis court. Specially created viewing platforms were installed at the far end of the parkland, so that walkers could stop to admire the newly created vistas of water and park.

The largest lake is crossed via a lawned, arched stone

bridge bordered with day lilies and taxodium trees. Randle had sandstone rocks placed in the water, adding to the impression that this landscape has been here for centuries. In the parkland about forty to fifty trees were planted, along with swathes of wild flowers and daffodils. The croquet lawn was created, marked out with architectural cones of yew. A cutting and vegetable garden was planted in the original walled kitchen garden, along with a small orchard. The driveway at the front of the house was improved with a circular turning area and a specially commissioned stone-urn water feature – an imposing finale for visitors arriving at the house via the parkland.

Offset from the new driveway is a double row of mature horse chestnut, beech and cherry trees, which dates from many decades ago. This screens the garden's more formal areas, adding to the sense of anticipation as to what lies beyond. The gardens adjacent to the rectory include a pergola walkway of white roses leading to a concealed sunken garden. Strategically positioned wooden seating areas in the parkland encourage walkers to pause and reflect on the romantic views to and from the house.

PLANTING

Randle worked with a specialist plantsman, Dr Martin Parham of Herbiseed, to create the wildflower areas in the parkland. Wild flowers thrive best in poor soil, so there is no point in planting them in places where nutrients are high; natural grassy areas are ideal. When the seeds are first sown, there are always one or two species that predominate, and it is important to cut these back quickly before they have a chance to seed; this allows the less aggressive species to establish themselves. It took about two to three years to achieve the effect that Randle and Martin wanted, using a combination of plug plants and specially harvested seeds.

The lush planting around the lakes includes many exotic day lilies and grasses, oversized crocosmia, white buddleias and hydrangeas, *Miscanthus zebrinus*, kniphofia and *Gunnera manicata*.

ABOVE LEFT: Clumps of brightly coloured day lilies border the lawned stone bridge that crosses the largest lake.
ABOVE: The sunken terrace is a connection that leads from the pergola walkway to the tennis court, which also provides a moment of magic and surprise for those who come across it unexpectedly.
RIGHT: An ornamental stone pedestal is the foundation for this bespoke water feature at the front of the house.
FAR RIGHT: The well-maintained croquet lawn adjacent to the house leads down to a further lawned area and the lakes beyond.

RESULT

The clients were overjoyed by the transformation, particularly as the lakes and parkland were fully established within a couple of years. As the trees mature over the years, the garden promises to give them even more pleasure. The house now has the presence it deserves, the landscape having been expertly manipulated to do it justice.

ABOVE: An artist's impression of the classical pedimented temple, which is in keeping with the romance and period of the house.
RIGHT: Planting alongside the lakes features swathes of miscanthus.

'The creation of a lake can only be achieved with a great deal of technical expertise. Not only is there the issue of how a lake will be filled, but it is essential that it be adequately lined. Without proper planning and preparation it would leak, emptying the lake and flooding nearby properties – something that would almost certainly result in costly legal action.

'Here lakes were dug and two boreholes were drilled deep enough to reach the aqua flow, in this case about 610 metres/2,000 feet (in fact only one was used). It is important that lakes are deep enough, both to prevent evaporation during hot weather and to keep them cold enough to deter the more pernicious weeds and rushes from taking root. The average depth here was 2.5 metres/8 feet.

'People often wonder how fauna and flora establish themselves in newly created lakes. In fact, it happens naturally. Ducks and other visiting birds bring spores of plants and other wildlife with them, which in turn thrive. Of course they also bring aggressive weeds too, such as duckweed, but these can be controlled. It does not take long for an ecosystem to build up once the environment is provided. The lakes here are alive with birds and huge dragonflies.'

PARADISE IN THE SOUTH OF FRANCE

'For me, half the satisfaction is in creating a garden of beauty and character. The other half is in seeing the client's joy at the result. I like to think this really is a little slice of Paradise.'

The interior designer Kelly Hoppen introduced Randle to this project in the south of France. The property had been built in the 1960s and had become very sad and unloved over the years. However, it had spectacular views over Tahiti Beach and the bay of St Tropez, and benefited from certain features typical of the region, such as parasol pines (*Pinus pinea*) surrounding its boundaries, an avenue of tall cypress trees and mature olive trees. There was also an old kitchen garden and a rather neglected swimming-pool area. The house is situated at the highest point of the property with gardens sloping down, in all about 2.8 hectares/7 acres.

LEFT: Mature parasol pines, in keeping with the locality, have been planted to frame the magnificent view to the sea beyond.
RIGHT: A path of French limestone has been built right around the property, softened with textural planting, including *Pittisporum tobira* 'Nanum' and chamaerops.

CHALLENGE

In order to complete the internal building work, the contractors needed two access points instead of the single one available. The garden sloped down from the house and the second route was to be built from the bottom corner of the property, so that lorries would effectively drive up the centre of the garden. The redesign of the garden had to be planned around this upheaval.

This was a second home, so the client wanted a garden that she would enjoy primarily from June to September, that offered space and activities for her teenage children and that would be in keeping with the house once it had been given a Hoppen redesign. In fact the biggest challenge proved to be finding contractors locally who would carry out the work to the required standard and deadline.

VISION

Randle wanted to create a design that made the most of the garden's natural attributes – its location, views and native species. There was no cohesion in its original layout, so he needed to find ways of making practical and aesthetically pleasing links from one area to another. It was clear from the start that terraces should be built on the slopes; he also planned a pergola walkway to connect the cypress avenue with the main terrace and entertaining area. An elevated walkway was also designed that maximizes both views of the garden and the stunning seascape beyond.

SOLUTION

In order to facilitate the second access route for the contractors, Randle implemented a scorched-earth policy and removed everything in its way. While the structural work to the house was being carried out, he concentrated on other areas of the garden, transforming the old kitchen garden – the only area that was already on a flat level – to a tennis court that could also double as a five-a-side pitch or basketball court. A traditional pétanque court was also created. Beyond the court, a greenhouse and nursery area

ABOVE: This smart new driveway was constructed from porphyry setts from Italy, banded with York stone from England.
RIGHT: Because of the hot climate, for the dry terrace Randle chose sun-loving perennials, shrubs and herbs such as French lavender, Corsican hellebore, thyme, cistus and verbena.

GARDEN | RANDLE SIDDELEY

were built, complete with custom-made composting bins to make the garden self-sufficient. The swimming pool was completely remodelled with imported Italian Botticino mosaic. At one end is an art wall, created by designer Tim Gosling, and at the other, a classic loggia with an awning for shade.

A path was built right around the house, passing through an attractive second terrace (under the first-floor balcony), which is dressed with rattan garden furniture complemented by gardenias and citrus trees in terracotta pots. This opens on to the main lawn, where mature parasol pines have been

planted to frame the view, and then to steps that descend to the swimming pool. Paths were also built down each side of the garden, with a pergola walkway of western red cedar to the left. This is dramatically lit at night with mirrored uplighters between stainless-steel supports. Beyond the swimming pool are more steps leading down to a lush tropical garden that replaces the previous woodland. A viewing platform captures views of the sea through the canopies of the trees.

Once the access drive was no longer needed and the main landscaping could be tackled, lawn terraces were built to replace the previously sloped garden. These required

ABOVE: A Modernist-inspired stone art wall makes an effective focal point for the pool and the landscape beyond.
RIGHT: Once created, the wall was rendered and then wittily and boldly decorated by the designer Tim Gosling.

FOLLOWING PAGES
LEFT: The end of the elevated walkway features this organic sculpture.
RIGHT: Olive terraces on the south-facing aspect of the garden are underplanted with swathes of aromatic lavender, agapanthus and tulbaghia.

retaining walls made with dressed stone in keeping with the region. While Randle did his utmost to find local contractors and artisans to carry out the walling, landscaping and specialist planting, the work was only finished in time by also assembling teams from the UK, who took over the gargantuan task of laying about 800 square metres/ 8,600 square feet of French limestone, plus a specially bound aggregate to stop paths slipping in the rain. A new driveway was laid using porphyry setts from Italy and York stone banding from England.

PLANTING

The avenue of cypress trees was replanted between the lawn and the swimming pool, underplanted with convolvulus. South-facing olive terraces have been planted with deep swathes of lavender, tulbaghia and agapanthus, so that when you look back to the house lavender appears to cascade down the terraces in one glorious wave. The dry garden terrace above the woodland part of the garden is planted with perennials, shrubs and herbs, such as cistus, salvia, artemisia, ballota, phlomis, sage and thyme. An exuberant mix of jasmine, wisteria, bougainvillea and

climbing 'Lady Banks' roses combine on the pergola walkway. The pétanque court is surrounded by bamboo, oak-leaved hydrangea and sophora trees, while the pool terrace is framed by pittosporum and cypress trees. Elsewhere in the garden, perennials including lavender, verbena, artemisia and nepeta have been planted, so that the client can enjoy the most colourful and fragrant flowers throughout the summer months.

RESULT

The client was extremely happy with the transformation: a beautiful garden in keeping with the spectacular local landscape, but which also offers leisure activities for the family when they are on holiday. Her words on seeing the garden were the greatest compliment: 'If there is a paradise, then I have arrived.'

'If you are employing local contractors to work on a garden abroad, don't rely on your knowledge of a second language. I am half-French myself, but I still employed my wholly French mother-in-law to translate all my notes from English to French each time I made a site visit, to avoid any confusion when issuing instructions to contractors. It is not only language that can be a problem but culture too. One of the issues that threatened to delay completion beyond the agreed time frame here was the amount of national holidays that occur in France during the spring, and a different interpretation by local workers of the idea of deadlines!'

OPPOSITE: This pergola walkway of western red cedar, lined with a row of identical terracotta urns, is covered with trachelospermum and wisteria.
LEFT: The urns have been repeated around the garden, making effective punctuation points between path and lawn.

A GRACEFUL SETTING

ABOVE: A view of the rear of the house, taken from the restored walled garden.
OPPOSITE: The driveway now sweeps elegantly through the parkland to the front of the house, creating a sense of arrival.

This handsome Georgian house in Dorset is surrounded by parkland and enjoys big, open views. The garden extends to about 3.2 hectares/8 acres, with part of an old walled garden to the rear of the property. The client had added an extension to the house and also wanted a pool area.

CHALLENGE

The house also owned an adjacent stud farm with various offices and outbuildings. The drive led past these unattractive buildings in a confusing layout, making it difficult for visitors to know which route they should take for the house. Ugly metal fencing also distracted from the parkland view.

The house itself was on a slope, so the front elevation was on a different level to the rear. In addition, the land sloped at each side. Randle had to find a way of preventing these various contours from fighting with each other.

VISION

Randle felt that the garden and surrounding parkland were not doing justice to the architecture and location of the house. He wanted to create a design that would look authentic to the setting.

SOLUTION

Randle re-routed the drive so that it now leads from the road through parkland to a gentle incline with a pleasing view to the property, before arriving at the house itself. In order to screen the farm offices and outbuildings, he dropped the level of the driveway slightly and built up a high bank on both sides. This is now planted with trees, which will mature over the years; in a few years' time, nobody will even be aware that the buildings are there. Fencing has been removed and

ABOVE: Redundant farm buildings provide the perfect backdrop to the new swimming pool. The holm oaks will add structure once mature.
RIGHT ABOVE: The swimming pool under construction. The rear entrance driveway can be seen on the right.
RIGHT BELOW: The original walled garden has been planted with deep herbaceous borders, edged with box. Oriental plane trees add vertical interest.

'The farm offices and stud farm were a major scar on the approach to the house. Now we have implemented a much more sympathetic design that will only improve as the planting matures over the years.'

overgrown areas of hedging thinned out, so that parkland views can be enjoyed to the full.

Randle located the perfect position for the swimming pool in an old courtyard area, with redundant stables all around it. These now provide ideal changing and recreation areas. Yew hedging and holm oaks have been planted to provide a screen as they mature. A series of terraces with wide steps has replaced the original slopes of the garden, flanked by wide beds of lavender.

Half of the original walled garden (which is listed) was still intact, but in order to bring a sense of order to the design, Randle had to introduce a level change to the side of the house where the extension had been built. Listed Building regulations prevented any disturbance to the original wall

foundations, so instead he built a retaining wall of railway sleepers and concealed these behind a hedge, which will mature over the years. The planting stops short of the sleepers, so as not to interfere with the foundations.

PLANTING

The walled garden area is framed by wide herbaceous borders planted with anemones, peonies, irises, thalictrum, echinops and other perennial plants. To the front of this planting is a border of oriental plane trees, which gives the vista additional interest. On the upper lawn is an avenue of amelanchiers, underplanted with lavender. The renovated stables around the pool terrace are clothed in 'Kiftsgate' roses and trachelospermum.

RESULT

The property was a confusing hotchpotch of buildings and levels but now the house sits elegantly and comfortably in its surroundings.

OPPOSITE: The swimming pool enjoys a sheltered and secluded position on the site of the old farm courtyard. 'Kiftsgate' roses now adorn the old stables.
LEFT: The herbaceous borders in the old walled garden include *Verbena bonariensis* and *Anemone japonica*.
ABOVE: Randle manipulated the landscape to create these gentle banks, creating enough room for a generously sized terrace.

'Railway sleepers are not the most attractive of objects, but they are ideal for situations such as this where land needs to be brought into control and prevented from moving. "What the eye cannot see . . ." is a good maxim. Hedging planted slightly in front is the ideal way of camouflaging the fact the sleepers are there at all'.

CITY

A garden in the city is both a privilege and a delight. London is blessed with acres of parks, but there is nothing to beat stepping out of your own kitchen or living room into an oasis of green and calm. Even a roof terrace or balcony can make all the difference to the pressures of urban living.

Few city gardens are without problems, though. Most are overlooked and overshadowed by other buildings, which reduce light and privacy. Often the garden is on a different level to the main house, so you either walk down steps from the ground floor or up steps from the lower ground one to reach it. Subterranean extensions have become fashionable in recent years, but these come with unsightly skylights and ventilation shafts. And nearly always urban gardens are on the small side. That means the designer's skill and eye have to be even keener than when creating a garden in acres of ground.

The three London gardens I have included here range in style from controlled and classic to super-contemporary. Each of them had very specific problems but were blessed with owners willing to go the distance creatively. Happily, I enjoy a challenge and I was delighted with what we achieved together.

LEFT: This city roof terrace has been ingeniously designed to provide zones for cooking, dining and seating.
RIGHT: Trellis screens of western red cedar adorned with trachelospermum provide privacy from surrounding properties.

AN ELEGANT SOLUTION

'There are a lot of issues that the eye does not see, but which have to be thought through at the planning stage, maintenance being one of them. It is all a question of thinking ahead.'

LEFT: Four clipped *Quercus ilex* form the centrepiece of the garden, separating the lawned area from the stone terraces.
ABOVE: Randle has diverted attention from an unsightly skylight with this gracefully curved stainless-steel wall, down which water cascades endlessly.

This garden in central London is about 30 x 20 metres/100 x 66 feet, slightly more generous than is usual. Interior designer Joanna Wood introduced Randle to the project. The clients wanted an elegant design, but also space for entertaining and a grass area where children could play. Changes of level had to be navigated, and a subterranean pool room and squash court had to be landscaped into the scheme too.

LEFT: Randle's original mood board for the garden, showing the Mediterranean influences that inspired the planting. RIGHT: The *Quercus ilex* trees take the eye from the house to the second water feature – the octagonal stone lily pool.

CHALLENGE

The challenge was to take a small but prestigious garden and give it a sense of depth and space, with various areas for family use. In addition, landscaping had already begun when the client received planning permission for a squash court to be built under the garden. Squash courts are double height – 8 metres/26 feet rather than 4/13 – so this was an enormous structural challenge: in effect a gigantic concrete box was to be sunk into the ground, on to which topsoil had to be reintroduced. The client asked Randle to design a skylight for the squash court that would not jar with the rest of the garden. Drainage is always an issue when you upset the existing landscape to this degree, so this had to be put right in order for new trees and plants to survive. With the garden being on different levels, it was also important to instil a sense of balance and harmony to the whole area.

VISION

In this garden, Randle was inspired by gardens of the Mediterranean, where emphasis is often placed on structure and leaf foliage, rather than beds of flowers. Water is also an attractive feature in such gardens, so he planned to include both a traditional lily pond and an ultra-chic water sculpture. He wanted the scheme to introduce very clearly defined areas of 'hard' and 'soft', with separate garden rooms for activities such as playing and eating.

'Water sculptures are an attractive addition to a garden. Here, one also serves the function of camouflaging an intrusive skylight. However, for such features to work well and to be easily maintained, it is important to think not only about how the tank and plant machinery can be hidden, but also about access to that machinery. In this case, manholes have been cleverly blended into the paving, under which the technical equipment is located. It is essential to make sure that such equipment is kept dry; it cannot be placed anywhere that might flood.

It is not only water features that present issues of maintenance. Irrigation systems need to be drained down, cleaned and restarted at least once a year. In addition, many people today enjoy their gardens by night as well as by day, so it is recommended to include a lighting scheme within the rest of the design, preferably one that is sophisticated and versatile. Light bulbs do fail, so you have to ask yourself whether you are going to replace them individually or whether it might be better to replace them all once a year. One of the advantages of LED lighting is that the bulbs last much longer.'

Paved areas feature a simple grid system of pale limestone and darker York stone, with trees carefully positioned to accentuate the chequerboard effect – leading to the garden's dining area.

SOLUTION

A glass conservatory with French doors was built on to the rear of the house, providing a new access point to the garden. At the core of the garden design is a simple grid system of pale limestone and darker York stone. Laid out on this is a traditional 'avenue square' of four clipped standard *Quercus ilex*, deftly framed by box hedging and black ophiopogon. At its centre is the hexagonal granite lily pond that Randle designed, which brings life and movement to the garden. An inviting seating area is discreetly screened from neighbouring properties by a backdrop of pleached lime trees and trellis, underplanted with wall-trained olives and purple heucheras. To the right of this (looking from the house) is a lawned area.

Steps lead down from the main terrace to a lower terrace, specially excavated to give access to the pool room and squash court. Randle designed a semicircular stainless-steel water cascade to hide the unsightly but essential skylight over the latter – a spectacular and architectural solution to the problem.

PLANTING

Around the perimeter of the garden is a simple colour scheme of creams, whites, blues and greens, including agapanthus, hostas, cornus, *Tellima grandiflora* and ferns, all complemented by miniature box hedging. The front garden has been transformed into a knot garden, using box hedging with topiary specimens.

RESULT

When the clients first saw Randle's proposal on paper they could not believe how big their garden appeared to be. The design is striking, but it is also comfortable and practical, with space for the children to kick a ball, a dining area and a formal garden: a bold statement in the urban landscape.

CAMOUFLAGE & CHARACTER

'People often wonder why even quite a modest-sized garden can be expensive to revamp, but you have to remember a garden is nearly always bigger than the footprint of the entire house. If it is not well designed, it will be an under-utilized space that does nothing to add to the desirability of a property. You can't take on a project such as this and implement only half of the redesign. A new garden should be seen on the same level as installing a high-end kitchen.'

This imposing house in south-west London had been developed about ten years previously, with a subterranean swimming pool and games room running underneath along the length of the garden. At the far end is a mews house used by staff. Randle was introduced to the clients by interior designer Kelly Hoppen. They had young children and wanted a garden that could be enjoyed by all the family, but which also reflected their Japanese roots.

OPPOSITE: Steps from house to garden feature have lights inset into the stone, providing atmosphere at night.
LEFT: The staff house at the end of the garden is now partly hidden from view by panels of western red cedar trellis.

CHALLENGE

The four skylights over the pool and games room resembled a line of unsightly flying saucers. A border of box and lavender, rather than screening them, had only served to draw further attention to how obtrusive they were. As if to accentuate this, a path had been laid centrally down the garden, leaving a strip of muddy grass to one side. The path led directly to the staff mews house, visible from the main house, with no privacy for people in either residence. Access to the garden from the house was via a cumbersome and ugly spiral staircase, with additional narrow steps up from the kitchen – an illogical arrangement.

VISION

When it came to choosing materials and planting, Randle took inspiration from the clients' desire for an oriental-style garden. He set out to create a simple yet eye-catching space

for adults and children alike, which would be a far cry from the existing scheme. He recognized that the success of a new design lay in imposing some structure, but with a light touch.

SOLUTION

First of all, Randle improved access to the garden. He widened the lower ground-floor terrace to make space for comfortable seating, and created wide shallow steps – visually centred from the new family living room – leading up to the main garden. A new separate staircase to one side now gives directly on to the lawn from the first-floor terrace.

Panels of cedar latticework, evoking Japanese Shoji screens, were used to hide the skylights, incorporating a small dining niche. This was further enclosed with a large planted area of mature Japanese maples and azaleas; their gnarled stems and bronze foliage are uplit at night. A wall

ABOVE: The original garden with its 'eye-balls' of box and lavender, and scrubby strip of grass to the right.
RIGHT: The same view now: the staff house has been gently screened by the bronze water feature, giving privacy on both sides.

of Japanese bamboo along one side was planted to provide immediate screening of the garden from its neighbours.

Randle's *pièce de résistance* is a stunning, huge curved bronze water feature with a shallow pool – about 3 metres/10 feet across – with a narrow reflecting pool. This creates a focal point at the far end of the lawn, and provides an elegant screen between the main garden and the mews house. Set against a yew hedge, the bronze wall conceals a small recreation area to its rear for use by staff and their children. At night, it is lit theatrically to spectacular effect, as is the rest of the garden.

PLANTING

Japanese planting is all about shape and texture, so the theme here is muted evergreens with domed, feathered and spiky foliage. Dwarf pines symbolize youth and longevity,

while azaleas and maples give a blaze of seasonal colour. Black grass was chosen as a contrast against the radiant hues of the bronzework.

RESULT

The clients were thrilled because their investment gave them everything they wanted from the garden – and more besides. Now, instead of looking out at four giant 'eye-balls', anyone visiting the garden sees a sophisticated but simple design of oriental planting, bamboo screens and the wonderful bronze water feature.

ABOVE: The skylights are now hidden by slatted screens.
OPPOSITE
Above: The curved bronze water feature, made to Randle's design, is a striking addition to this Eastern-style garden.
Below left: Water continually circulates up from the pool to cascade over the top once again.
Below centre: Uplighters in the base of the water feature illuminate it to spectacular effect.
Below right: With sympathetically chosen light fittings the garden takes on a theatrical character by night.

'In small city gardens, solid paths running centrally up a lawn are very obtrusive. Stepping stones are a subtler solution, allowing you to take a normal stride over wet grass rather than being reminded of a mini motorway. They are also easy to maintain, as you can run a mower over them. In this garden, York stone has been used to edge the flower beds, a pleasing way of stopping the edges of a lawn looking messy. As plants grow, they will cascade over the borders, adding to the visual effect.'

GARDEN | RANDLE SIDDELEY

AN IMAGINATIVE APPROACH

These clients own the ground and lower ground floors of a period house in west London. The garden is large for a city house – about 18 x 20 metres/60 x 66 feet – and situated on a corner plot. At some point in its history, it had been laid out with a central lawn area, flower beds filled with shrubs to each of the three boundary walls and a path going around each of these. It was a very old-fashioned arrangement and made the whole space seem much smaller than it actually was.

ABOVE: A contemporary garden pavilion provides a second seating area and helps screen the garden from the adjacent road.
RIGHT: York stone slabs edged with gravel are complemented by herbaceous plants, including lavender, erigeron, nicotiana and astrantia.

CHALLENGE

There were various structural considerations to take into account before a redesign was possible. First, there was a big sycamore tree against the boundary wall between the rear of the garden and adjacent neighbours. It was important that whatever works were carried out should not disturb the tree, because if it were to die the roots would decay and shrink, resulting in voids under the ground, which in turn could cause structural damage to the neighbours' property. The second problem was that one of the boundary walls was in danger of collapse. Structural engineers were needed both to assess what had caused this and to advise on how best to rectify it. The third consideration was that staircases leading up from the lower ground floor and down from the ground floor effectively blocked out views from all the windows on this elevation. Once all these issues were solved – and the correct Listed Building permissions obtained – it was a question of creating a garden design that would do justice both to the property and to this elegant corner of London.

VISION

Randle wanted to create a city garden that would offer attractive views both from the house and from the garden itself. One of its most special features was that when you are in the garden, it is possible to enjoy wonderful borrowed views by looking across the adjacent properties in the same street; you can catch glimpses of about eight other gardens, each with different trees, structures, shrubs and styles – the equivalent of looking out over about 0.4 hectares/1 acre of green, pleasant space in the heart of London. In order to capitalize on this spectacular asset, Randle wanted to open the garden up, still keeping a generous grassed area but without the walkway and the density of the shrubs.

SOLUTION

Structural engineers investigated the failing wall – which had been propped up over the years – and found that another tree dying some time ago had caused the damage. They found the original wall foundations 2 metres/7 feet below the surface and rebuilt the wall from these, doing away with the need for props. Randle also redesigned the access into the garden, by moving the stairs so that they ran from the ground floor down to the garden from the side of the house – as opposed to cutting across the front. As a result the view to the garden was hugely improved. On the lower ground floor, he designed a much deeper terrace area about 5 metres/16 feet deep where the clients could have a table and sun loungers. Beyond this, wide stone steps lead up to the lawn. He also had a contemporary pergola built to one side of the garden: this looks out over the adjoining gardens, making the most of the borrowed views, while giving privacy from the adjacent side road. It features comfortable seating and an open fireplace, providing a memorable *al fresco* experience.

Once the structural problems of the boundary wall had been solved, Randle removed nearly all the existing planting, beds and paths, so as to begin with a clean canvas. Sandy York stone was used for hard areas, and retaining walls were

'Taking on a redesign of this scale, particularly in London, requires great project management. Not only did the success of this project rest on the specialists used – building consultants to help with Listed Building consents, structural engineers, pavilion architects and specialist growers – but there were also various services to co-ordinate as well – water, electricity and gas (for the fireplace in the pavilion). A fast-approaching fiftieth birthday was the unmissable deadline, which made it even more important that not a day be wasted. If you are able, seek specialist help for project management at the beginning and build any additional professional fees into your budget.'

OPPOSITE: A view of the original garden with the protected sycamore tree. It was a mass of unruly shrubs with no underlying design.
LEFT ABOVE: Lawn and flower beds have now been brought back under control. The sycamore has become a pleasing feature and there are borrowed views into adjoining properties.
BELOW: The bespoke wall of water, made from stainless-steel louvres, adds sophistication and wit to this contemporary design.

GARDEN | RANDLE SIDDELEY

'Circumstances do not always permit that you carry out work in the recommended order. Applying for Listed Building consent invariably means time delays, which we could not afford, given the tight deadline. So we submitted our proposals and plans, and carried on with work that was unlikely to be seen as contentious while we waited for the planner's verdict. One thing that helps in such a situation is if you have good relationships with your immediate neighbours – as these clients happily did.'

rendered in a colour sympathetic to this. Stepping stones leading from the stairs coming down from the ground floor to the lawned area are more subtle and unobtrusive than the previous solid paths; pebble borders give them additional contrast. Planting was chosen for the beds that would provide colour and interest for the majority of the year.

Randle worked with the specialist Andrew Ewing to create a bespoke water sculpture at the far end of the garden. This comprises fine sheets of brushed stainless-steel louvres with serrated edges, floating on an infinity pool of black granite. Concealed LED lights have been used to illuminate the cascading water, creating an amazingly hypnotic effect. Not only does it look beautiful but it draws the eye down the length of the garden, accentuating the feeling of space. It is set against a backdrop of tall grasses, hydrangeas and a newly planted yew hedge – all chosen so as not to disturb the sycamore tree.

PLANTING

In order to achieve an instantaneous transformation, Randle employed the services of a specialist grower, Crocus, who offers an incredible selection of plants at all times of the year. The lawn is bound by richly planted herbaceous borders, including peonies, bronze fennel, salvias, ornamental grasses, agapanthus and irises. This planting is complemented by two mature specimen *Cornus kousa* set in boxes planted with buxus, a multi-stemmed amelanchier and a mimosa tree. Clay pots on the terrace are planted with olive trees.

RESULT

The clients are blissfully happy, particularly as they had not realized just how much potential the garden offered until they saw it completed. It was finished just in time for one of their milestone birthdays, so a huge marquee was erected over the whole area – from the water feature to the back of the house. Visitors thought the flowers were for the party only, so were even more impressed and delighted when they realized they were part of the actual planting scheme.

ABOVE: The new terrace features a high-tech barbecue, cooking area and wine storage for *al fresco* entertaining.
RIGHT: Lit at night the water feature becomes a spectacular work of art, the focal point of the garden's design.

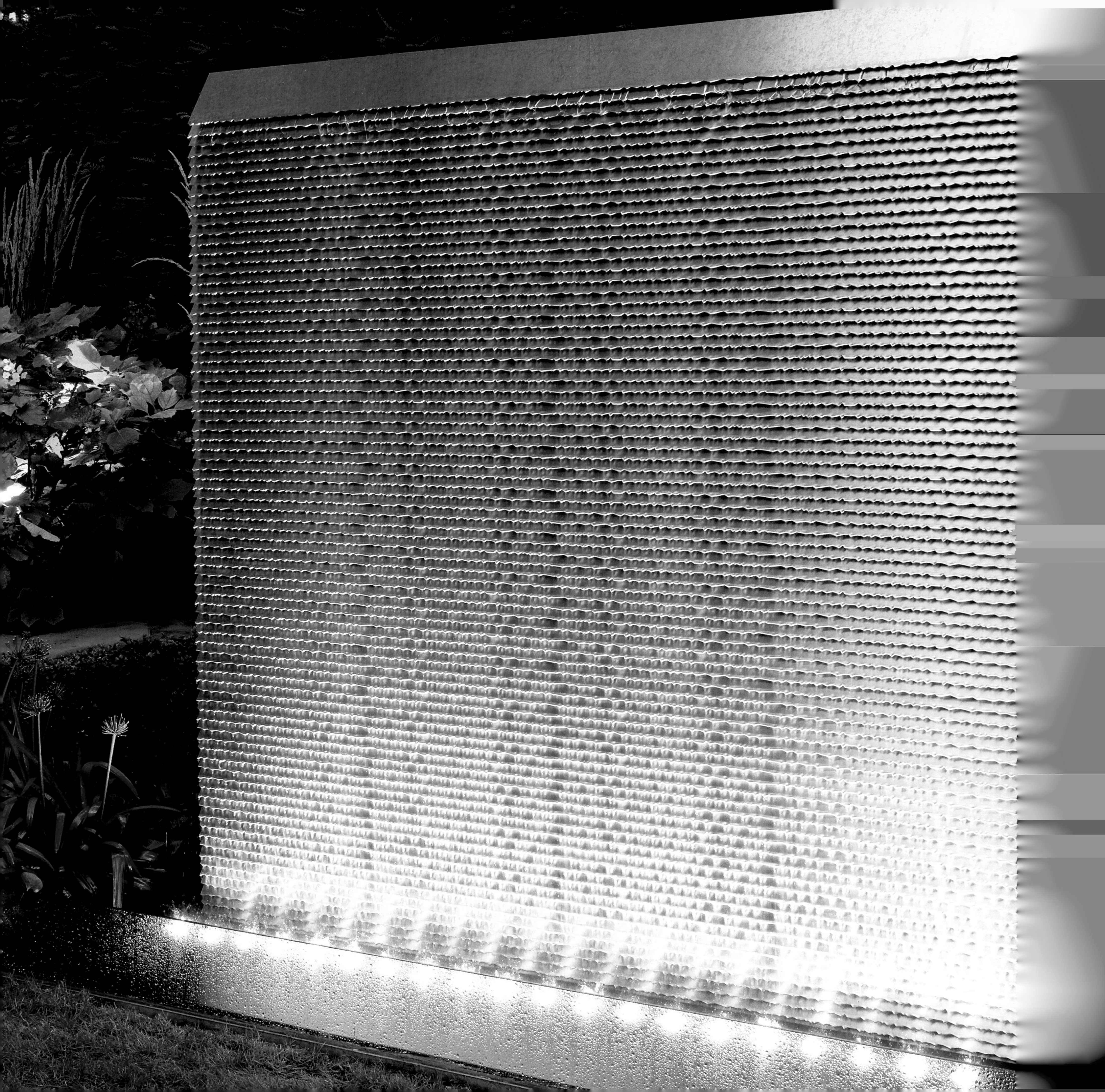

PLANTING

When I look at a plant, I try to envisage how it will be all year round. It may be a beautiful lady when dressed in fine clothes, but is it also a beautiful lady with nothing on at all? For me, the foliage is the important thing, whereas the flower is the icing on the cake.

I love to see how plants change over the seasons: the way the leaves change colour and eventually drop; the surge of growth in summer and the dying back in winter; the full glory of colour in summer – like an orchestra playing a crescendo. I imagine myself as a composer planning where to add melodies and harmonies. For those of us who live in truly seasonal climates, it is such a pleasure to watch a garden transform over the months. First come the bulbs, from the snowdrops of late winter to the daffodils of spring; then there is the blossom – the magnificence of the magnolia and the hazy white cloud of apple trees; on rolls summer, with the full flowering of the herbaceous border and the rose garden; even autumn remains beautiful as the leaves change into myriad shades of gold and red. And if you have also chosen plants for structure as well as seasonal display, the garden will continue to look beautiful through winter, particularly when draped in snow.

The important thing is to understand how each plant will work with the others. There is no need to be over-complicated when creating a planting scheme: some of the best are very simple in terms of colour and species. Think of plants as musical notes: as one disappears another one takes over. It is all a question of scale, balance and harmony.

Plants such as ornamental alliums have been planted to encourage bees and therefore pollination, essential for a healthy garden.

PLANTING AS STRUCTURE

Planting can add just as much structure to a garden as walls and paving do. You can opt for structured hedging, such as yew, box or beech. You can plant an avenue of trees to create a grand entrance, be it lime trees in England, cypress trees in Italy or palms in Lebanon. And if you are fortunate enough to own a country estate, you may well have magnificent parkland trees within the landscape that draw the eye around the view.

It is also possible to impose structure on otherwise rambling plants by using timber pyramids, obelisks or pergolas, on which you can grow climbing roses, clematis, jasmine, sweet peas or other flowering plants.

I have a particular fondness for plants such as amelanchier. When bare stemmed, these create strong vertical lines, but the tops can be trained into a hedge of fluttering leaves and abundant white flowers. Other favourites include standard trees, such as olive and rose, clipped *Quercus ilex* and bold ornamental grasses.

Small city gardens are particularly suitable for using plants as a key element of the design's strength and structure. In the country, it is often a question of looking at existing trees and hedges and deciding how best to integrate them into the new design of the garden.

PLANTING FOR COLOUR

Everyone has personal preferences of colours. My own taste is for soft blues, greens, yellows and whites. I don't usually opt for very bold colours, although one bright red rose bush in the distance can give a welcoming punch of colour that draws the eye forward. As a general rule, plant bolder colours further from the eye and softer ones nearer – a shade such as pinky white is impossible for the eye to read if it is too far away. Don't mix too many shades at once, either: if you are planting camellias, for example, choose ones that are either

white or red. If you plant a mix of white, red and pink, you lessen the impact rather than adding to it. Planting should be a bold brushstroke.

Strong colours work best in small city spaces, such as roof terraces and even window boxes, where you need something vibrant against brick and stone. In most gardens, there are moments of high drama – in June and July – and then much quieter times to each side of these. Personally, I like that change of tempo. Choose specimens that give changing displays of colour, such as hydrangea, which go from green to pink to rusty red.

Of course many plants offer wonderful scents as well as colours. While I would not want to be overpowered by floral fragrances in the garden, it is lovely to catch the scent of jasmine, rose or lily-of-the-valley as you walk through a garden. Plant heavily scented specimens at intervals so that they do not fight with each other.

BUYING PLANTS

The golden rule is: do not buy in haste. Garden centres and plant nurseries are tempting places, but if you have a limited budget you should buy one spectacular tree or shrub rather than a variety of ground-cover or herbaceous plants. You need to understand how much space your specimen plants will take as they grow and then fill in around them, rather than trying to work backwards. Buy herbaceous perennials in groups of odd numbers – three, five, seven, nine; even numbers never work so well. Remember that you can split herbaceous plants in the autumn, so you can fill out your garden year on year in this way without having to spend a fortune at the garden centre. It is all a matter of patience and continuously assessing what works best where.

TREES

If you are fortunate enough to have some wonderful mature

species of trees in your garden, make the most of them; you could even light certain ones at night for dramatic effect. Trees are also useful for screening out other people's properties or unsightly views. Remove them at your peril: not only are many rightly protected, but they can leave a much larger gap in the garden than you may have envisaged. If roots are dug out, land subsidence can follow many months later, which could be extremely detrimental to your new garden.

If you long to have more trees to add vertical structure, textural foliage and interest, it is worth budgeting for some fully mature specimens. Although costly, even one or two trees can make all the difference to a garden. And who really has the patience to wait several years for a sapling to grow into something magnificent?

In my own projects we have craned in many tree specimens over the years, from palm trees in the Middle East (see page 42) to pleached pear and lime trees (see pages 164 and 165) and mature magnolias (see page 189). Often I use them to emphasize the structure of the garden, as with the line of cypress trees in the south of France (see page 6) or the planes that edge the herbaceous border on page 118. Trees may change from season to season, but they are one of the constants of the garden's structure, as beautiful in the depths of winter as in the height of summer.

LAWNS

For many people, a garden is not a garden without a lawn. However, be practical. If you have a small city garden, overhung by trees and overshadowed by neighbouring properties, a lawn will struggle to remain healthy. Grass needs plenty of sun and ventilation. You can take up the existing lawn and returf with a new lawn that is bright green and fresh, but within months it will look just the same as the old lawn if the conditions have not changed.

Even in a big garden with sun and air, a lawn needs constant maintenance – not just regular mowing, but weeds removed by hand, scarifying (which removes moss), aerating, topdressing and regular reseeding. Don't overwater the lawn; once a day is enough. If you water too much, you won't encourage the roots to dig deep, looking for moisture. Grass is a plant like any other: it needs a good strong root system to survive. An overwatered lawn will be the first to turn yellow when there is a drought, because the roots are not strong and deep enough.

Because lawns are demanding of time and care, some of my clients ask for Astroturf. This can be suitable for gardens where children play and an all-weather surface is required, but don't think that they are always the answer. An Astroturf sample will look pristine – just as a turf sample will – but once it has been outside for a few months suffering the elements and accompanying wildlife, it will look very different. I really only advise its use in gardens where a real lawn has no chance of growing.

'Think of plants as musical notes: as one disappears another one takes over. It is all a question of scale, balance and harmony.'

Don't be too regimented when planting. Here, salvias, alliums, bronze fennel, *Rosa* 'Charles de Mills' and peonies planted in swathes look wonderful and create the perfect habitat for beneficial wildlife.

SCHEMES OF HARMONY & MELODY

For many people, plants are what makes a garden – all those temptations at nurseries and garden centres – but in fact they are more akin to the soft furnishings in a house. They are the colour and texture that are added at the final stages of a design, the floral equivalent of cushions and throws.

Of course every garden I design has individually created planting schemes, based not just on the colours and species that the client favours but also on the soil, climate and aspect of the particular garden. Although many people love certain plants so much that they try to grow them regardless of the conditions, the fact is that it is best to be inspired by the plants and trees that are indigenous to the area.

This is something of particular importance in the gardens I design internationally, where a great deal of research is often necessary in order to ascertain exactly which species we should introduce and which to avoid.

The three gardens I have chosen here needed first and foremost a great design concept, as all landscapes do. They range from a new-build in New Jersey to a period villa in the English suburbs to a classic London town house. The planting schemes we created for them were as individual as the clients and locations concerned. I like to think they may offer some inspiration to those who love the joy of flowers and foliage.

A colourful display of day lilies,
campanula, echinacea and phlox
borders an avenue of clipped
hornbeam.

OLD WORLD MEETS NEW WORLD

'In situations like this, where the driveway leads past garages or outbuildings before arriving at the house, it is important to make it clear to visitors where to drive to and where to park. Here a retaining wall and ornamental side gate were introduced to shield the garden from view of the drive, indicating that you need to keep going until you arrive at the front of the house. The clients were originally reluctant to remove the driveway island, thinking people would park immediately outside the front door. In fact, the subtle change of hard surfaces makes it clear where cars belong.'

This traditional white-boarded house in New England is in fact a new-build which was bought by American clients who had lived for some time in England and wanted to recreate an English-style garden here. They were introduced to Randle through designer Paolo Moschino of Nicholas Haslam Ltd. Situated deep in a valley and surrounded by protected woodland, it is in an idyllic spot. However, the house did not sit well within its location originally because the developers had spent only the minimal money required on landscaping.

ABOVE: An attractive wrought-iron gate connects the side of the house to the gardens. RIGHT: The weather-boarded exterior of the new house. Low box hedging and clipped yew create an attractive entrance to the property.

CHALLENGE

Access to the house is via a driveway, entered from a road high above the house. Originally, the first view of the house was of its roof – not its most attractive feature. The driveway approaches the house from the rear, so it was not clear to visitors where to stop and park. Because the land slopes, drainage was also an issue. Every time there was heavy rainfall, water would collect in big pockets on the driveway and in the garden. The woodland is habitat to deer, which are not friendly to young plants, as they love to eat green shoots. Planting was also a challenge, as the weather in New Jersey rotates from very hot summers to extremely cold winters, unlike the more moderate climate of England.

VISION

Randle decided to replace the slope with a series of connecting terraces and garden rooms, each with its own character. These would include a herbaceous avenue, an

151 area of lawn with a pétanque court and an avenue of clipped hornbeam. He also saw the necessity of re-landscaping the swimming-pool area to include a more attractive pool house that would reflect the architecture of the house and conceal unsightly pool equipment. The entrance to the house needed a total rethink, as originally it had been designed around an old-fashioned island, which detracted from the house's handsome architecture.

SOLUTION

Randle produced the design for the new garden, but a local contractor was employed to implement the designs. The client became project manager, which was a crucial role in such an ambitious project. Drainage was the biggest problem, but under Randle's guidance this was solved by digging deep trenches, about 1 metre/39 inches in depth, at the side of the driveway and filling them with shingle – French drains, in effect. Land drainage was also installed at 50-centimetre/20-inch distances to feed excess water into these trenches.

The client already had an interesting collection of antique garden artefacts and contemporary garden art, and Randle made sure these were integrated into the terrace garden rooms. For example, an eighteenth-century Swedish urn stands at the end of the herbaceous avenue. A bronze horse's head by the sculptor Nic Fiddian-Green takes pride of place on a plinth positioned within a semicircle of conifers, while an antique lead trough has been placed against an ornamental wall at the far end of the pétanque court.

Tall conifers were planted along the driveway, making an effective screen. Now there are intriguing glimpses of the house, but no complete view of it until you arrive at its door. Deer fencing and a cattle grid were installed to prevent deer from entering the garden area. The pool area, garaging and entranceway were all re-landscaped, using moss-lined brick and stone, to achieve a more harmonious and attractive effect.

'In a garden with drainage problems on the scale of this one, it is crucial to employ the right contractor. Ideally look for someone with experience of building golf courses. If you don't get it right, the site will become too waterlogged to allow new plants to grow, and grass will turn yellow. The right project management is also essential. At RSA, we usually project manage our own schemes, but in this case, the client had experience of working in interior design and decided to take the job on herself. She really did have to put a great deal of time and effort into doing so and without that commitment, the outcome could have been very different.'

LEFT: The eye is drawn down a wide herbaceous avenue to the eighteenth-century Swedish urn at the end.
ABOVE: The dining area has been created in between the different garden levels, affording views in several directions.

In addition, a new family terrace was designed for comfortable outdoor eating, complete with outside kitchen and barbecue.

PLANTING

Randle sourced the plants from local New England nurseries and from Canada to ensure that all plants would be accustomed to the climate here. Lavender, for example, was sourced from a specialist local nursery and planted only against warm, south-facing walls. Hornbeams and yew came from a nursery in Ontario. Many of the trees and herbaceous plants were grown especially to order, including the hornbeam trees and box hedging. The hornbeam avenue is bordered with beds of lilies, alliums, hellebores, bergenias, geraniums and foxgloves. The rich herbaceous border is a masterful blend of species such as oriental poppies, lilies, campanula, acanthus, salvias, delphinium, aquilegia, alliums, hosta, geranium, hellebore and sedum.

Lavender, wisteria, roses and clematis strike a romantic note elsewhere in the garden.

RESULT

This is a house that looked uncomfortable within its setting but now appears to have been there for ever. It is a pleasure to see it so transformed, especially as the client herself worked so hard to make it happen. The whole family are delighted with the garden and love everything it offers in terms of relaxation, entertaining and amusement. In a recent letter to Randle, the lady of the house wrote: 'We cannot tell you how much we love the garden and quite frankly, we spend more time out of doors, than in, even when it's blisteringly hot . . . We cannot thank you enough for all that you've done to transform our ridiculous house into something sublime. I never thought I would feel this way, but I would be sad to leave the garden anytime soon.'

ABOVE: A hornbeam-lined
path creates a vista from the
front entrance of the house,
each tree underplanted with
a square of box hedging.

RIGHT: The children's play area features this wonderful tree house in the woodland that borders the garden.
BELOW RIGHT: The bronze horse's head by Nic Fiddian-Green is the focal point of the pool-house area.
FAR RIGHT: Access to the tree house is via a rope bridge, adding to the sense of fun and excitement.

TRADITIONAL FAMILY VALUES

'In a period house and garden, it is tempting to try to hang on to every original feature. Beyond the courtyard garden here was a series of old, dilapidated greenhouses that were no longer functional. I persuaded the clients to allow me to replace these with new ones, which at first they hated, preferring the shabby chic of the original. However, once they were brim full with an abundance of plants and exotic edibles, they quickly changed their minds. The moral is to always allow your eye to adjust to something new. Big items, such as garden buildings, require time to "bed down". '

This family home is situated in a suburb to the north of London, a green-belt area that links the city to the countryside. It is a nineteenth-century Arts and Crafts house of red brick, exposed timber and ridged tiles. The clients had extended the house, building a larger kitchen and children's play area with a swimming pool and gym on the level below. Interior design firm Todhunter Earle introduced Randle to the project. The enormous garden – about 2.4 hectares/6 acres in all – included an old walled kitchen garden and a large pond, but other than that was mainly a big exposed space, with no sense of surprise or secrets.

LEFT: At the front of the house, Randle planted two *Quercus ilex* in the newly created York stone and gravel parking area, while two benches flank the gate leading to the main entrance.
ABOVE: The top terrace features cedar planters containing twisted-stem bay trees. The steps are surrounded by box planted in a loose cloud formation.

CHALLENGE

Although parts of the garden had been re-landscaped before Randle was approached, what was needed was a big vision for what could be achieved, to give interest and structure to the whole space and realize its true potential. The clients requested a design that would complement both the new-build areas and the original Arts and Crafts architecture. It also had to be extremely child friendly, while offering adult relaxation and enjoyment as well.

VISION

Randle wanted to inject the garden with some magic. It is built high on a slope, with borrowed views of trees and green spaces beyond. He planned a scheme of garden rooms that would allow visitors to discover parts of the garden as they walked through, rather than seeing everything on first view. The front garden was also in need of major renovation.

LEFT: The twisted-stem bay trees are underplanted with dwarf white lavender, a classic combination that adds character to the terrace.
FAR LEFT: The front garden features traditional herbaceous borders, interspersed with evergreen oaks. Plants include alliums, bronze fennel, irises and aquilegias.
RIGHT: A walkway of *Betula utilis* var. *jacquemontii* is underplanted with foxgloves, lupins, pachysandra, crambe and various ornamental grasses.
BELOW RIGHT: An artist's impression of the woodland walkway.

SOLUTION

The front of the house was accessed via a driveway that was routed past common land and ended in a big open space in front of the house, but with nothing to physically separate the drive from the house. The first thing that Randle did was plant two *Quercus ilex* in the parking area, providing a visual link to the four he planted alongside the path leading to the front door. He also placed two benches against the low wall that divides the front garden from the parking area. These have a practical use – somewhere to rest shopping bags or children's sports equipment when unloading the car – but more importantly, they soften the hard landscaping and make it appear instantly more homely. Gravel on the drive has

been replaced with York stone, which continues all around the property. New flower beds edged with box hedging have been planted in the front garden to reflect the lines of the building, while walls have been softened with climbers.

To the rear of the house there is a small courtyard garden, which is accessed from the kitchen. The clients wanted a traditional English country garden here, with lots of colour and textural foliage. Randle planned a surprise for them: when they went away for ten days, he enlisted the help of specialist growers, Crocus, and incredibly the clients returned to an English garden in full flower. They had no idea how instant a garden can be. Randle also designed a water feature, in collaboration with Andrew Ewing, for the

LEFT: The old kitchen garden has been transformed into a cutting garden for flowers and herbs. Today the pergola walkways are festooned with roses.
ABOVE: An artist's impression of the same area. Rose varieties chosen include 'New Dawn' and 'Climbing Iceberg'.

courtyard; when lit at night, this adds interest and theatre. In the main garden, he designed a stepped water rill that links the main garden to the pond.

The terrace leads down to a croquet lawn and then to the garden beyond. Here there is a walkway of silver birches that looks particularly eye-catching from the house. In addition to this woodland walk, Randle planted a cutting garden of flowers, herbs and bulbs in the old kitchen garden – a feature the clients love – with rose-covered pergola walkways along the boundary walls. A new orchard has been created. There is also a delightful, slightly wild water garden planted around the existing pond. Finally, he gave the children a fantastic play area at the bottom of the garden with cricket nets, a trampoline embedded into the ground and 'flying fox' wires.

PLANTING

The front garden features traditional herbaceous borders filled with alliums, irises, bronze fennel, astrantia, aquilegias and rose varieties such as 'Glamis Castle' and 'Boule de Neige'. These borders are edged with box and punctuated with topiary evergreen oaks. In the courtyard, climbing roses and trachelospermum clothe the walls, while herbaceous perennials such as Japanese anemones, *Salvia nemorosa* 'Caradonna', *Stachys byzantina* and *Lavandula stoechas* spill out over the paving.

On the upper terrace are cedar planters of twisted-stem bay trees and pots of olive trees, each underplanted with different lavenders. *Geranium* 'Philip Vapelle' and *G.* 'Johnson's Blue' make a stunning display at the base of the oak pergola, on which climbers, such as roses, wisteria and *Vitis vinifera* are trained. In the cutting garden, varieties such as *Hemerocallis* 'Gentle Shepherd', *Iris sibirica* 'White Queen', gypsophilia, phlox, alstroemeria, sweet peas and *Rosa* 'Winchester Cathedral' flourish.

The birch walk is underplanted with woodland-style planting, such as ferns, bulbs and ornamental grasses. Roof-trained amelanchiers, again underplanted with swathes of ornamental grasses, lead down to the water garden. Here species such as acanthus, stipa, geranium, bergenia and foxglove have been added to the existing plants.

RESULT

The garden is now a space that all the family can enjoy to the full. Not only that but it marries the Arts and Crafts architecture as well as being in harmony with the contemporary extension. Rather than being one big open area, it has been transformed into a series of rooms, each with its own unique character and charm.

'If you are fed up with building work and long for a garden to be finished, there is an argument for splashing out some of the budget to give yourself one area of "instant" planting. Within ten days, we achieved something here that looked like Chelsea Flower Show. It really gave the clients a much-needed boost.'

ABOVE LEFT: A rill echoes the line of the steps that lead from the upper garden to the pond.
ABOVE: In the wilder part of the garden, amelanchier trees are underplanted with ornamental grasses, ferns and spring-flowering bulbs.
RIGHT: The children's play area features a fantastic tree house, with tyre swing, slide and embedded trampoline.
BELOW LEFT: The bespoke water feature in the courtyard garden is made from limestone and designed to be enjoyed at night from the house.
BELOW RIGHT: Randle has designed the garden as a series of interconnecting terraces. This view looks from the lower gardens back towards the house.

AN OASIS IN LONDON

'This is an example of clients thinking a garden could do with a simple makeover and then being persuaded that more drastic action was needed in order for it to fulfil its true potential. Once they saw the design drawings, they understood the merits of such action. I hope I have done justice to the original garden, while also transforming it into a place of pleasure and beauty through harmonious planting and judicious choice of materials.'

This is a narrow London garden, measuring about 20 x 7 metres/66 x 23 feet, that had previously belonged to fashion designer Hardy Amies. He had used L-shapes of pleached dwarf pear trees to instil structure and create privacy. The house had since been sold to a young Swedish couple with small children and dogs. They wanted to use the garden primarily for entertaining and favoured a traditionally English style of garden. Randle was introduced to the project by the interior design division of Colefax & Fowler.

ABOVE: This cascade of water, surrounded by agapanthus, links one section of the garden to the other.
RIGHT: At each level of the house, bespoke standard trees have been used to make a visual connection with the formal garden below.

'If you have children and dogs, it is tempting to hang on to every last patch of grass in the garden. The problem is that – particularly in a garden with a lot of shade – grass is often damp and unattractive. In addition, it looks unsightly if stained by dog urine. A hard surface, such as the marble gravel used here, is not only easier to maintain but imprints a city garden with sophistication and a timeless elegance. Add softness with planting, ideally a combination of flowers, shrubs and herbs.'

GARDEN | RANDLE SIDDELEY

CHALLENGE

Randle wanted to do justice to a garden that had been well designed many years ago, but also to move it into the twenty-first century. As with many London houses, the different levels of entry to the garden presented problems. Previously the clients had accessed the garden from the lower ground floor and walked up to the terrace, unable to walk from the ground floor directly into the garden. On the left-hand side, the boundary retaining wall was beginning to fail. The garden had the benefit of mature trees on its perimeter, but these had grown rather wild and out of control.

VISION

Although the pleached pears were attractive in summer, they had no foliage in winter, so the garden lacked structure for half the year. Randle decided to complement these with something less changeable, while retaining the existing L-shapes. He aimed to emphasize the core structure with stone, gravel, water and lines of espaliered lime trees. The idea was to give the garden a strong spine, while also linking it harmoniously with the house.

SOLUTION

The pear trees were removed and transplanted to a specialist nursery, for nurturing while the garden was being re-landscaped. Transplanting trees is a risky business and

LEFT: A bird's-eye view of the garden shows the formal structure that Randle has imprinted on to the design, using half-standard clear-stemmed olive trees.
ABOVE: Replacing grass with marble gravel has accentuated the classical style of the garden and complements the planting palette of greys, greens and purples.

only four of the dozen or so survived, of which Randle replanted two. The retaining wall was rebuilt and the garden restructured into different levels. Now it is possible to walk from the ground floor directly on to the terrace. From this, steps lead down to the rest of the garden. Randle introduced clear-stemmed standard olive trees, which follow similar lines to the previous design. The existing small amount of grass has been replaced with a crushed marble gravel, more practical for a family with dogs. A formal water feature introduces a visual pause between the formal garden and a second more informal entertaining area at the far end of the garden underneath a mature fig tree. Water has also been used here for *feng shui* purposes – something the clients requested – so at the top of the fountain sit two oriental cats, which are said to ward off evil. Pleached lime trees help to maximize privacy, while also emphasizing the integral design of the garden.

PLANTING

The entire scheme is built around combinations of purple, green and the grey of the stone. This palette works at all times of the year and at all times of day. Half-standard olive trees create the inner garden. Beyond is the water feature, around which agapanthus cascades. On the flanking walls are espaliered lime trees underplanted with herbaceous perennials, primula and heuchera, for seasonal colour and interest. Climbing varieties include jasmine, clematis and solanum. Huge bay trees in planters have been placed on the bedroom balconies to connect visually with the formal garden below.

RESULT

This is a garden that is peaceful and calming, even though it is located in central London. It is the perfect place for entertaining friends and colleagues, but also offers plenty of space for family living. Classic Heveningham furniture completes the look.

AWKWARD SPACES

After all these years of designing gardens, I could say that every one is awkward in its own way. However, there are particular challenges with small city gardens: issues of light, privacy, level changes, neighbours, towering boundary walls and endless planning regulations. The key challenge to designing one well is trying to pack a lot into a very restricted space. Even a modest roof terrace will often require a table and chairs to be fitted in, neighbouring terraces to be screened out, a focal point in the form of water or sculpture, plants for all-year interest, lighting and drainage.

Good design is essential when space is at a premium; otherwise you will end up with a cluttered, disorganized look. Two of the biggest problems are often entry points and traffic routes. In a small garden on a different level from the house, stairs are necessary but will hugely cut down the available space. You have to see whether you can improve the layout in any way. You also have to think about how you will move around the garden, where the table and chairs will go, creating a pleasing vista when looking from the house to the garden and also the view looking back towards the house.

Having built up something of a reputation for solving awkward-sized and irregular-shaped gardens, I was spoilt for choice when it came to selecting some for this chapter. They are all in London, but in character and style could not be more different. The fact is that most of us experience the constraints of a city garden at one time or another, so I hope that you will find some of the solutions created here both informative and inspiring.

Even the most modest-sized garden can be manipulated to provide space for relaxing and dining, as at this city apartment.

A TALE OF TWO GARDENS: I

'Good design is about treating every garden differently, no matter how small. There are always ways of making something feel truly individual.'

This lower-ground-level garden belonged to an interior designer and her husband. The gardens in this part of London are often small and rather claustrophobic – this one measures only 5 x 10 metres/16 x 33 feet. Originally, it had some grass and paving, with a minimal amount of planting, but there was nothing to set it apart from the many properties surrounding it. On the plus side, it is a fantastic suntrap.

ABOVE: Balls of clipped box, some in urns, provide year-round interest in a garden with very little space for planting.
RIGHT: Priority was given to providing an outdoor dining area, so as to make maximum use of the garden throughout the warmer months.

This bird'-eye view of the garden shows how green tiles have been positioned to denote the dining area. The slim border of grass is a witty addition.

'In a garden such as this, with tall boundaries and restricted ground space, the trick is to concentrate on planting vertically. Here I created a corridor of green walls, which took away the oppressed feeling of being overlooked and created additional planting opportunities in a garden with little space for flower beds. The vertical was also emphasized with the timber artwork on the rear wall.'

CHALLENGE

Privacy was an issue, as houses on each side overlook the garden. There was also an unsightly back wall at the rear, which dominated the garden space.

VISION

Randle aimed to create a garden that reflected the clients' tastes, in particular their love of contemporary design. He recognized it was also important to imbue it with its own individual character, but to keep it as low maintenance as possible.

SOLUTION

The clients wanted an oriental feel, so Randle designed a garden that was predominantly stone and bamboo. A combination of hard surfaces – paving, decking and green-glazed tiles – create the foundation of the design. York stone squares have been set diagonally as a foil to the central diamond square of western red cedar decking, separated by a green tile border. Randle designed a slim border of grass between the tiles and the decking – a witty reference to the clients' desire for grass in such an impractical space. In fact they loved this boutique touch and replaced it on an annual basis. Trellises planted with climbers were used to extend the height of existing boundary walls.

PLANTING

Soft landscaping has been kept to a minimum, with small flower beds in the garden's four corners planted with ornamental grasses and clipped box balls. However, climbers were used in abundance, including jasmine, clematis, trachelospermum and solanum – a pleasing and sweet-scented way of giving the garden more privacy.

RESULT

The design achieved everything the clients wanted it to – an attractive oasis of privacy in the heart of busy London, which also reflected their own taste.

A TALE OF TWO GARDENS: II

'The biggest eyesore of the original garden here was the huge back wall to the rear. By making this a frame on which to hang artwork – the spectacular water sculpture – I transformed a bad point into a good one. Similarly, the idea of designing a bridge to improve the way the garden was accessed and used was pivotal. Always look for the solution rather than dwell on the problem.'

LEFT: Space has been maximized by creating a garden on two levels. The upper part is planted with architectural cypress trees, which take up little room.
RIGHT: The lower ground floor is mainly for the children's use, so safety gates have been fitted to prevent them from straying.

This is the house the same clients moved to a few years ago, by which time they had two small children. Again it is in Chelsea and again a very modest-sized space – at about 5 x 8 metres/16 x 26 feet, even smaller than the previous one. It had a mature bay tree and a tiny lawn, but nothing of particular visual interest. Like many such gardens, it was accessed by stairs leading up from the lower ground floor or down from the ground floor.

174 This view of the garden shows how the upper and lower levels connect via stairs and a custom-built bridge leading from the main house.

'Although this is a garden where you can sit
and have a drink on a summer's evening, it
is really designed to be seen from the house
at night – and to reflect what is happening
internally. I see it as a practical family space
by day, which at night transforms itself into
a work of art.'

CHALLENGE
The clients wanted better access to the garden both from the lower ground floor – which was the family space where the children played – and the ground floor. Although small, the garden had to provide some play space and an entertaining area, while reflecting the contemporary style of the house internally.

VISION
Randle wanted to achieve a design that would give the garden cohesion, while also catering to the family's needs. He also wanted to create something eye-catching that would be in keeping with the clients' collection of contemporary art and their own strong sense of design.

SOLUTION
On the lower ground floor, there is a conservatory with French doors. A small garden with a sand pit was created on this level where the children could play. Randle then designed a bridge to lead from the ground floor to the main part of the garden – a dramatic feature, which is also highly practical. To accentuate the note of theatre, he designed a stunning water feature that is the focal point of the garden by night. This is constructed out of finely woven stainless-steel mesh panels, hung like curtains, with water cascading down the central panel. When lit at night, it looks like a work of art.

Niches and recesses in the wall are fitted with uplighters, enhancing the experience and atmosphere. Additional trellises have been added to the boundary walls to improve privacy.

PLANTING
This was designed to emphasize the architecture and theatre of the space. The palette is composed of Italian cypress trees, tightly clipped box hedging, black-stemmed bamboo (*Phyllostachys nigra*) and trachelospermum. The existing bay tree was kept and clipped into a more sculptural, oval shape. As with the previous garden, the planting has an oriental feel, with screens of bamboo used to hide the unsightly party wall at the rear. Raised planters have been used to compensate for poor soil depth.

RESULT
The building of the bridge and installation of the bespoke water sculpture made this scheme complicated to build, but the clients were thrilled with the result. The chic garden they now own is a far cry from the dull and ordinary space they originally inherited with the house – a truly modern design that will add value to their property should they decide to move again.

EAST MEETS BEST

'The western red cedar screens made all the difference – it is as though a big arm has been wrapped around the garden, giving a sense of comfort and calm. I have taken on some challenges in my time, but the success of this redesign was nothing short of a miracle.'

This garden is on the lower-ground-floor level of a London house, so it is to all intents and purposes a basement courtyard. It is overlooked by surrounding properties and tiny in comparison to the house itself. Originally, the only feature of merit was some established camellias.

ABOVE: Looking down on this compact garden, it is possible to see how the change of flooring clearly delineates one zone of the design from another.
RIGHT: Slatted screens of western red cedar wrap around the perimeter, creating a feeling of privacy and intimacy.

VISION

Randle set out to create a sunken, city garden that is warm and comforting, with plenty of Eastern influences to reflect the client's nationality.

CHALLENGE

The space itself was very unpromising: it was dwarfed by high, dark walls and had been paved with ugly engineering bricks. The main entertaining area in the house is on the ground floor (the floor above the garden), so there had to be views from here as well as access to the garden via a metal staircase. The garden is also accessed via the lower-ground-floor kitchen. In such a small garden – about 7 x 5

metres/23 x 16 feet – these entry points presented additional complications.

SOLUTION

Randle screened the unattractive boundary walls with a slatted screen of western red cedar, about 4 metres/13 feet high, which embraces the space and provides a feeling of privacy and security. Decking denotes a sitting area, giving the impression of a room within a room. Rectangular stepping stones lead from the pathway and planting to outdoor sofas. The property walls have been painted a creamy colour, creating extra warmth. External lighting ensures the garden remains an attractive oasis by evening as well.

ABOVE: The high cedar screens both minimize ugly views to neighbouring properties and imprint a style signature onto this Eastern influenced garden. RIGHT AND FAR RIGHT: The garden under construction. Using screens to create a room within a room made an enormous difference to the atmosphere.

'The choice of garden furniture is another way of stamping a signature style upon a garden. These contemporary outdoors sofas by Dedon, with padded cushions, accentuate the feeling that this is an outdoor room to the house, a continuation of the living space. A row of tall contemporary planters against one wall complements the furniture perfectly and emphasizes the core structure of the design.'

PLANTING

Randle managed to preserve most of the camellias and then introduced structured planting, rich in foliage and texture. Semi-mature *Cornus controversa* has been planted in opposing corners to balance the scale of the existing camellias. The planting has to be shade tolerant and to look interesting at all times of the year: the mix includes evergreen ground-covering species such as luzula, euphorbia and pachysandra. Larger evergreen shrubs were planted to give structure and help to soften the walls, including autumn-flowering camellias, osmanthus and sarcococca – the latter two both having the added benefit of a lovely scent. Hydrangeas, ferns and hostas add rich texture with their foliage. Stepping stones have been interplanted with baby's tears (*Soleirolia soleirolii*).

RESULT

The garden has been absolutely transformed from a cold and hostile space surrounded by high, dark walls to an area that is both relaxing to sit in and pleasing to look out on.

A CITY JEWEL

'Sometimes you have to be cruel to be kind. The growth in this garden was simply suffocating and I cut an incredible amount away, to the clients' initial horror. However, a year later you would never have suspected that it had undergone such radical surgery.'

The clients' favourite thing in this Chelsea garden was their perfume-bottle-shaped swimming pool. This took over the larger part of their bijou garden, which measured only about 6 x 15 metres/20 x 50 feet in total.

LEFT AND RIGHT: The perfume-bottle-shaped swimming pool is the starring feature of this tiny London garden. Pots, urns and spirals of topiary add to its exotic character.

Randle cut back plants, trees and shrubs, restoring control and order to the garden's design, while retaining the effect of its being an oasis of greenery.

'The shape of this pool is unusual and attractive, but it raises questions of practicality: it needs a custom-made cover, as without a cover the expense of heating the pool would make it very environmentally unfriendly. Covers are advisable, both for retaining heat in pools and for keeping debris out. Thin plastic covers can be a problem because they trap rainwater, which then pushes them down into the water. The safest are those that are fixed to the edge of the pool. When I design a pool, I include a recessed edge all around so that such a cover in effect sits on a ledge, making it far more stable. The ledge would not prevent someone from falling in, but it would give them valuable time to shout for help.'

CHALLENGE

Because of the swimming pool, the flower beds were very narrow and trees, shrubs and plants were fighting for root space. The whole garden had become out of hand. The pool equipment was housed in a Gothic-style building that had become dilapidated, with a mulberry tree growing virtually into its walls. The clients wanted to emphasize the feeling of seclusion by blanking out the roof of a neighbouring property to the rear.

VISION

Randle recognized that the design of the garden itself could not be changed because of the pool, but he wanted to bring it back under control in order to make the best of the garden's many charms.

SOLUTION

Severe pruning was called for. Over the course of two to three days, Randle cut back trees, roses and shrubs with ferocity. The clients initially hated what they saw, but he told them to wait a year and then they would enjoy the difference. He also persuaded them to have the pool house remodelled in the original romantic design. Horizontal posts and cables were used to cover the roof of the neighbouring house and climbers were trained over these; within a few years, these will cover the roof entirely in greenery.

PLANTING

This is a garden with colour and interest all through the year. It is intensively planted, so that as one thing dies down, another one takes star billing. Randle specified a wide range of herbaceous plants, shrubs, roses, bulbs and climbers, including aquilegias, astrantias, gaura, irises, agapanthus, anemones, hydrangeas, roses and lavender. Climbers were selected for scent as well as foliage, and include trachelospermum and 'Iceberg' roses. Pots, urns and twists of topiary add to the garden's exotic character.

RESULT

The clients were tremendously happy to see the garden reborn through tender loving care and expert pruning. It now complements the pool perfectly, making the garden the ideal urban oasis.

A SENSE OF ORDER

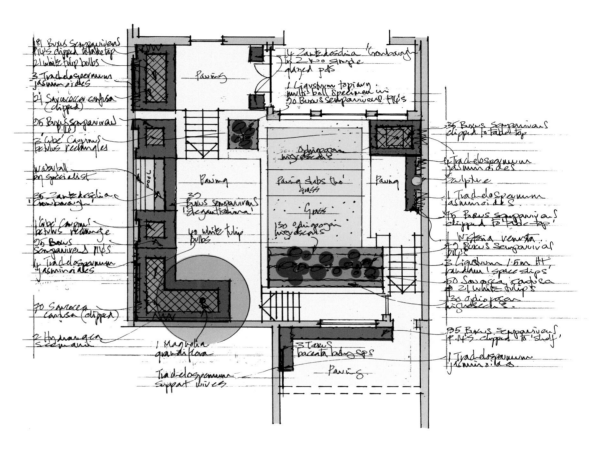

LEFT: Each level of this small but complex space seems to link seamlessly with the next, achieving a sense of balance and harmony.
ABOVE: Randle's plan and notes show how difficult it was to transform such an unpromising space.

Located in the heart of Chelsea, this bonsai garden was a test of Randle's design skills. The property developer who commissioned him, Willy Gething of Property Vision, wanted to marry the new-build house with an adjacent mews house. The latter was to be used as guest accommodation and required access to the garden from both a studio room upstairs and a lower-level bedroom. Access from the main house was via the kitchen-dining room on the lower ground floor. Even though the garden was so tiny, it was part of the brief that there should be a terrace area for sitting and dining. Structurally, the garden had to meet strict weight constraints, as it is built over an underground car park.

'London is made up of small spaces like this one where it is essential that every element works perfectly from a practical point of view and that it all ties in together. This design is successful because it brings balance to all the disparate ingredients.'

PREVIOUS PAGES: Randle harmonized the impact of existing arches by using them to frame the bronze water feature he designed as a focal point on the lower level. Cloud-clipped *Ligustrum jonandrum* provides year-round interest, complemented by box, zantedeschia and *Ophiopogon planiscapus* 'Nigrescens'.
LEFT: The cloud-clipped *Ligustrum jonandrum*, with views to the conservatory.
OPPOSITE: Views down to the rear entrance to the main house.

FOLLOWING PAGES:
LEFT: Bronze was chosen as the material for the water feature, because it complements the London brick of the surrounding walls. Trachelospermum softens the feature's edges.
RIGHT: The subterranean car park meant that planting had to be kept to the perimeter of the garden, because of weight issues and the availability of planting depths. Stepping stones link the two areas.

CHALLENGE

The tightness of the space, a total of about 10 x 10 metres/33 x 33 feet, was the biggest challenge. There was also a huge wall to one side, about 10 metres/33 feet high, which towered over the garden. In addition, there were problems to overcome relating to the many access points at different levels in such a restricted area. The design had to bring unity to a very complicated layout and make good use of the few opportunities there were for planting.

VISION

Randle's aim was to create a magical 'secret' garden, which would have a real 'wow' factor and not feel at all claustrophobic. The immense wall was a problem, but it also provided him with inspiration because of its arches. He recognized that these could become part of the structure of the design.

SOLUTION

Randle designed a water feature in bronze to be placed against the central arch of the wall. Bronze, rather than stainless steel, was chosen, as it is a subtler colour in a garden of this size. The design of the feature is simple, with water cascading down into a trough before recirculating.

Framing the water feature are bands of rectangular yew, which soften the effect of the wall's height. A terrace of 5 x 3 metres/16 x 10 feet was constructed in front of the water feature; this is edged with York stone, which matches that of the stepping stones over the lawn.

PLANTING

Specimens of huge *Magnolia grandiflora* were craned in for an instant effect and to screen surrounding buildings. Other more architectural plants, such as clipped ligustrum and cloud-clipped yew, provide visual impact and year-round interest. The water feature is framed by columns of yew and trachelospermum. Clipped box, hostas and arum lilies complete the architectural style of planting. Weight-loading issues (because of the car park below) meant that planting had to be kept to the sides rather than the centre. There is barely any soil depth: because soil weighs significantly more when wet, it had to be kept to a minimum.

RESULT

The garden's design has proved its success by adding value to the house and giving it an additional important selling point. Successive owners have been so happy with it that it remains untouched five years after its installation.

'Simplicity is the key to a design such as this. Here, a carefully considered mix of limestone and York stone ensures stairs, terrace and garden all sit happily together. I removed existing chunky balustrades on the stairs and stripped out other cruder architectural elements.'

'Like so many people, these clients had not realized how much potential was lying dormant in the garden they had owned for many years. Once they agreed to the bold step of allowing me to strip it down to basics and begin all over again, I was able to give them a garden that surpassed all their previous expectations.'

REVAMPING THE EMPTY NEST

This family garden in west London was in need of a total transformation when Randle first visited. It had been a place for children's games and family pets, but with the children now growing up, the parents wanted to reclaim it as an additional relaxing and entertaining space for them. The family also wanted a dedicated storage area for wine to be integrated into the design. Catherine Connolly of Northwick Design introduced Randle to the project.

ABOVE: The space here has been completely reconfigured to provide zones for seating and dining on two levels.
RIGHT: Randle's original artwork shows how he conceived the design, including seating set into hedges of mature yew and box.

CHALLENGE

The garden had no real structure and was not organized in a practical way. Rather than make cosmetic improvements, Randle persuaded the clients to allow him to rip it all out and begin again. Walls urgently needed repairing and rebuilding before any new work could commence.

VISION

Even though the garden is modest in size – about 20 x 6 metres/66 x 20 feet – Randle could see that there was potential for a series of 'rooms' for sitting, dining and wine storage. The change of levels between these spaces would be defined with low, wide steps.

SOLUTION

Randle designed a scheme that is simple but visually strong. The basement family room has been visually extended via French windows to an outdoor living room, with two generous outdoor sofas placed opposite each other. The drab, dark grey York stone paving was replaced with 'floorboards' of limestone to relate to the wooden-floored interior. The pale stone lightened the formerly gloomy aspect and created an interplay between outdoors and indoors. The sofas are set into a deep, clipped hedge of mature yew; shortly after planting, this dense green backdrop appeared to have been there three years, rather than three weeks. Generous box 'side tables' were planted on either side.

The hedge continues onwards, drawing the eye up the steps to the middle terrace, recreated as a dining area. A pair of standard hollies was retained here and two further

matched hollies of perfect size and form were sourced. This intimate space is now defined by strong balls of foliage at its four corners. External power was provided to enable the hollies to be lit with fairy lights at Christmas, a seasonal delight for small children and adults alike.

Further wide steps lead to the third terrace, which is home to the garden's focal point, a sinuous curved bronze water wall. This is placed centrally and backed by a hedge of copper beech, whose red and gold autumn foliage enhances the effect of the water shimmering off the bronze metalwork. A screen of trelliswork frames the view from the house to the water feature and also serves to hide a specially constructed garden building, which contains the client's wine collection. A gate leads into communal gardens beyond.

PLANTING

Tall trellis panels were installed right around the garden, camouflaging a mishmash of garden walls and fencing. This provided an elegant framework for new planting, so the garden is now an oasis of greenery. Trachelospermum, rambling rose 'Phyllis Bide' and clematis furnish the trellis with flowers and provide wonderful scent, particularly in the evening. The planting palette in the upper terrace was mainly bronzed foliage to complement the water feature, including the slate-coloured grass ophiopogon, the spiky charcoal leaves of *Phormium* 'Platts Black' and red-foliaged *Berberis* 'Helmond Pillar'.

ABOVE: By clipping yew to echo the shapes of the outdoor sofas, Randle began to imprint a signature style on to the previously unruly garden.
OPPOSITE (top to bottom): The garden under construction – razed to the ground first and then rebuilt to the specified design.

RESULT

The former tired and muddled arrangement has been replaced by a smart city garden of three rooms that make an attractive continuation from the house. The clients had initially been reluctant to place two large sofas on the small terrace, but these transformed their enjoyment of the garden. An effective but subtle lighting scheme allows them to curl up here and relax or read on warm, summer evenings. They were also amazed at the space they had once everything was stripped out. Today they use the garden through the greater part of the year, at all times of the day and evening. This garden was awarded a BALI national landscape award on its completion.

'In a garden of any size, it makes sense to build in storage areas for items such as seat cushions and parasols, so that soft furnishings can be protected from rain if need be. Here, I included two low storage boxes in the design at either side of the dining table, housing cushions and other garden paraphernalia. When dressed with vases of flowers or candles, they accentuate the feel of an elegant dining room.'

SOLUTIONS NOT PROBLEMS

'This garden's level is lower than the water level of the nearby canal, so good drainage was essential. A sophisticated system of pumps and French drains was installed to protect the garden from flooding. A common mistake when installing new gardens is not allowing for water to drain away from hard surfaces. If installing a paved terrace, make sure that it is designed so that water easily and naturally drains into the garden, rather than collecting in pools on its surface.'

LEFT: By building a pergola to the side of the conservatory, Randle visually extended the house, creating an attractive *al fresco* garden room.
RIGHT: A stone path now meanders around the boundary of the garden, where the new planting is rich and lush. The leopard adds an exotic touch.

This property is near a canal in central London. The lower ground floor leads down to what is in effect a sunken garden. The ground floor leads out into a small terraced area that was overshadowed by an enormous tree. The original design was very plain and uninspiring, with stepping stones cutting through the centre and no co-ordination between any of its elements.

GARDEN | RANDLE SIDDELEY

CHALLENGE

The water table is unusually high here, which created all kinds of problems with drainage. A huge tree had grown right up to the side of the building, threatening its stability. There was an existing conservatory that needed to sit more happily with the garden, and a retaining wall with massive buttresses that was far too obtrusive. That the client holds a Christmas party here every year and wanted to be able to cover the entire garden with a marquee was a further constraint on the design.

VISION

In a city garden of modest dimensions – this is about 20 x 50 metres/66 x 164 feet in total – it is fun to give a sense that there is something to explore beyond what you first see. The previous layout was all about getting from A to B as quickly as possible – hence the stepping stones slicing through the unimaginative postage stamp of a garden. In contrast, Randle wanted to create a design that takes the visitor on a slower, more circuitous route, screening off some areas from others and so imbuing it with a sense of discovery and mystery.

SOLUTION

First, the drainage had to be radically improved. This was an expensive job, but essential in order to transform the space through better design. Planning permission was granted to remove the tree on the grounds of safety; this brought more light into the garden and made it possible to create a much bigger ground-floor terrace. Randle designed a pergola that was built at the side of the conservatory, and York stone provided unity throughout the scheme. Stone is also a practical solution in a shady garden.

Yew hedges and Himalayan birch trees were planted to provide plenty of screening, while the flower beds were reshaped into curves. A stepping-stone path echoes their contours. The buttresses of the retaining walls have been softened with plenty of green foliage and flowering climbers. Now the garden can be enjoyed from both the lower-ground and ground-floor levels, while a professional lighting scheme makes it visually pleasing at all times of the year.

PLANTING

Randle planted camellias, which are ideal for shady spaces and look striking in spring against the yew hedging and the line of Himalayan birches. A selection of ornamental grasses provides year-round interest. These also complement a bronze leopard sculpture the client commissioned, positioned so that it appears to be stalking through the grass, about to pounce on its prey. The borders of the garden feature a rich and exotic tapestry of tree ferns, ornamental bananas, Chusan palm trees, evergreen oaks and black-stemmed bamboo. Ground-cover plants complement the pink and white palette of the camellias.

RESULT

The garden has been transformed from a nonentity of a space into a magical oasis. It is a relaxed and comfortable area for entertaining friends, and practical enough to place a marquee over its entirety for the annual party.

'There is no rush to walk around a garden. A path straight over the lawn may be the quickest route, but it is certainly not the most attractive option. Be more discreet and enjoy the fact you may not see the whole of the garden at once.'

Himalayan birches are a feature of the newly planted beds, complemented by tree ferns, ornamental grasses, echium and phormium.

'In a city scheme, it makes sense to use as many borrowed views as possible. Here, we had an abundance of trees and garden spaces in the vicinity which complemented our own design.'

A SHARED SPACE

RIGHT: Contemporary square urns planted with arbutus and *Convolvulus cneorum* have been used to separate the lawn area visually from the paved areas. OPPOSITE: A low square reflection pool and cascading water feature create a tranquil atmosphere in this busy corner of London.

AWKWARD SPACES

This is a commercial development in Chelsea, London, by Taylor Woodrow. The communal garden was tiny, about 8 x 24 metres/26 x 79 feet. The development is situated in a conservation area, and the garden design was an integral part of the successful planning application.

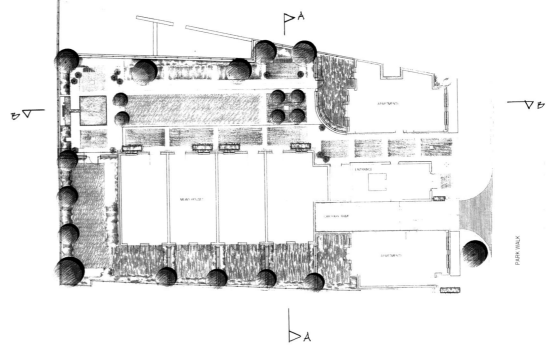

VISION

The garden was overlooked by the mews houses and apartments that surrounded it, but Randle wanted to make it feel as though it were a private town-house garden. He felt it needed a contemporary style that would reflect the crisp, clean architecture of the buildings.

CHALLENGE

An underground car park the length of the garden has ventilation outlets that needed to be visibly minimized. The tightness of the space also presented problems, as did the lawn depth of only 15 centimetres/6 inches.

SOLUTION

Charcoal-grey granite setts, contrasted with pale limestone slabs, provide the clean, contemporary canvas on which the garden is created. The same pale stone has been chosen for troughs and urns, designed by Randle, in which agapanthus and lavender are planted. The raised lawn distracts attention from the air vents (for the car park below), which run alongside the flower beds. At one end of the garden is a pair of overscaled square urns; these are echoed by a matching pair, which provide a marker between the lawn and the small stone seating area. Here, there is a stainless-steel water feature, cascading down one wall. This feeds into a low, square pool, which reflects the sky and trees. The presence of water in the heart of the capital is both visually pleasing and aurally comforting; at night the water is illuminated for additional effect. A specially commissioned statue by Dan Archer creates a focal point, which is visible from the adjacent street.

PLANTING

Along the southern boundary of the garden is a wide herbaceous border featuring trained amelanchiers set in tightly clipped frames of box hedging. Perennials include astrantias, aquilegias, miscanthus, sedum, thalictrum and panicum. Urns are planted with strawberry trees (arbutus) underplanted with *Convolvulus cneorum*.

ABOVE FAR LEFT: Grey granite setts are complemented by pale limestone troughs planted with lavender and white agapanthus.
ABOVE: Randle's original design shows how the mews houses link to the communal gardens behind.
RIGHT: Dan Archer was commissioned to carve a sculpture to complement the surrounding area.

RESULT
This is a communal garden that gives real pleasure to residents. It may be small, but it is in constant use throughout the warmer months.

'The colour of the stone you select is an instant way of imposing a style, be it traditional or contemporary, town or country. The combination of very dark granite and very pale limestone was ideal in this chic, urban environment.'

LIGHTING

204 A garden has many faces. It changes from winter to summer; rain to sun; snow to mist; early morning to late afternoon. Lighting the garden at night adds another aspect of its personality; it provides an opportunity to create interest and drama of a very different sort than daytime will allow. On a practical note, lighting also allows you to extend your use of the garden from summer to autumn, and from early evening to late at night.

So important is lighting that I commission the help of a lighting designer from the very first meetings I have with clients. Lighting is an essential component of the design concept, not something to be added in further down the line. It doesn't matter whether a garden is large or small, country or urban: the way it is lit is an essential part of its success and the total enjoyment it will offer its owners. One of the lighting designers for whom I have most respect is Sally Storey, design director of John Cullen Lighting and Lighting Design International, and she has kindly agreed to share some of her own advice and expertise here, for which I am very grateful.

At night, the drama of the pergola is created by small spotlights concealed at a high level, lighting down the posts on the right-hand-side. Small uplights in the base of the posts reflect off mirrors to light across the path. In the distance, uplights spiked in the planting uplight the façade. Good garden lighting, as with the interior of a house, is made up of combining various types of lighting at different levels – whether uplight, downlight or side light. It is balancing each of these effects that provides the magic.

LIGHTING THE GARDEN

Lighting is a versatile and highly effective tool of design. It can add colour, accentuate texture, create atmosphere and introduce drama. In the garden, it has the practical use of delineating pathways, highlighting steps and illuminating outdoor dining spaces. In addition, it increases the feeling of space from rooms within the house that enjoy a view of the garden. Plate-glass windows are like mirrors at night, but when the garden beyond them is lit, they are transformed from black rectangles into vivid tableaux. For a conservatory, or any room with large windows, lighting the garden is particularly important. No wonder, then, that lighting is increasingly recognized as a powerful additional layer of garden design. However, there is a great deal more to the art of good lighting than installing a few fittings suitable for outdoor use. The key is to orchestrate a successful balance between what is lit and what is left in shadow.

DESIGNING YOUR LIGHTING SCHEME

First, think about how you want to use your garden at night. Also consider the different areas and the permanent features within these, such as paths, terraces, trees, planting beds, water, sculpture and so forth. Approach your scheme in the same way you would an indoor room, including layers of light for general illumination, task lighting and highlighting focal points. The only thing different about designing garden lighting is that there is no ceiling; the same tools of light

LEFT: The temple structure against a wall is dramatically uplit using a 1W LED 'Lucca' uplight. I designed this to have a warm light with a twelve-degree narrow beam uplight to match the effect that had previously been achieved with 20W low-voltage uplights.
RIGHT: The theatrical effect of this sunken garden at night comes through playing dramatically with light, using only LED sources, with the focus being the temple structure against the wall.

are at your disposal, including uplighters, spotlights and the idea of silhouetting. There is less need outside for high levels of general light – you certainly want to avoid ending up with a garden that resembles a football stadium – so place the emphasis on decorative effects. A garden is more magical when you create a sense of mystery between lit and unlit areas.

The first thing to consider when creating a lighting scheme is aspect from the house. You need to light something in the immediate vicinity of the window, so that the eye is drawn past the glazing. Even illuminated flower boxes on a terrace achieve a new sense of depth and space. You then need to think about lighting something further into the garden which can become a focal point – a tree

BELOW AND RIGHT: Detailed areas of the sunken garden show how the latest LED technology of 1W Hamptons has been used to light the steps. I have selected olive-green fixtures so that when spiked into the planting they disappear in the day.

GARDEN | RANDLE SIDDELEY

perhaps or a piece of sculpture. The further away it is, the bigger the sense of space from indoors to outdoors you will create.

Even security lighting can be designed to be part of the lighting scheme as a whole. Instead of bright spotlights being triggered by movement, certain circuits can be programmed to come into play if something is detected. This has the advantage of appearing as though the lighting is being controlled by someone within the house.

CITY VERSUS COUNTRY

In urban gardens, the aim is to create a sense of the garden being an additional room of the house. It is about emphasizing space and depth. In a big country garden, it would be absurd to try to illuminate the whole area – and in addition would kill the beauty of a starry night; the trick is to highlight key elements of the landscape, such as particularly sculptural trees, a walled garden, a folly, gazebo or lake. The secret of lighting a big garden successfully is knowing when to stop.

What is important is to avoid glare. Consider arriving at a country house in the pitch black with a front door lit by a pair of bare lanterns outside: the effect would be very harsh. If you introduce some soft lighting around the perimeter – perhaps positioned within the planting or around a tree – and reduce the strength of the lanterns, you will create a far more inviting and relaxing mood. One of the most effective solutions is to introduce a small gravel pit within a flower bed, so that recessed uplighters can be hidden by planting but will not become submerged by it. Baffles or cowls can also be used to reduce the glare of lamps; this is particularly important with spiked lights.

The same approach goes for the rest of the garden. And don't use a few over-bright light fittings dotted about: think of ways of gently joining up soft sources of light throughout the garden. The aim is to create something magical and inviting, with a few well-placed moments of drama.

LAYERS OF LIGHTING

By day, you can enjoy the whole wealth of your garden. At night, you can discover little elements of it, and it is that sense of discovery that makes it so seductive. People can find their way by relatively low levels of light, so a gentle glow close to paths and garden routes is enough. However, it is important to have stronger light at changes of level, particularly steps.

Lighting focal points is also important to create atmosphere. It is not enough to install a lighting source: you also have to consider the direction of light. For example, you might have a very sculptural tree which will look best when uplit, and another one that you can light with a moonlighter, high within the branches, projecting light downwards and creating wonderful dappled patterns. Dense planting, such as box balls or hedging, looks best when lit in silhouette, whereas open foliage is more effective uplit.

Even the most subtle focus lighting can make an incredible difference to the way a garden looks by night. Arbours overhung by a vine or a canopy of clematis take on a soft glow when spotlighters are concealed in the foliage. Flowers in bloom can be lit with carefully positioned LED spots, which bring out the true colour of the plants. Uplighters through foliage create textural patterns of light and shade, particularly effectively against a wall. A statue at the furthest point of the garden takes on new character when uplit.

When planning your lighting, remember that seasons and time will make a difference, so the location of spiked lights may need to change. Deciduous plants and trees take on a very different appearance from winter to summer, and views change from year to year and season to season.

DINING AT NIGHT

When it comes to entertaining areas, such as terraces, think of these as individual rooms and try to mark them off from the rest of the garden. Pots can be useful demarcation objects. The trick is to have very gentle background lighting,

This loggia is an outside room with an open fireplace, providing a wonderful place to sit. At night the discreet copper fixtures located at high level give the timber slats a dramatic impact.

complemented by focus lighting over the table. You want the light to be bright enough for guests to be able to see what they are eating, without being overly intrusive. As with the lamps outside the front door, the aim is to have lights that appear to be illuminating the entire area but which are in fact subtly supported by other light sources. You might, for example, hang lanterns over the table, but keep these pleasantly dimmed, with additional lighting coming from uplighters within the planting at each side. Candles and garden flares provide an additional level of interest; try backing up the gentle flicker of candlelight with a concealed spotlight overhead. The lighting in your dining area should be balanced with lighting a few metres away – perhaps a lit tree or area of planting. Lighting one feature in the distance gives a visual focus and provides interest.

ENTRANCES AND EXITS

The entrance to your house should provide a welcoming reception. With a large house, the first view may be the gateway at the beginning of a drive, so it is important that this signposts the way for visitors without being too blinding – uplighters illuminating gateposts are very effective.

When it comes to deciding how best to light the front door, choose fittings in keeping with the architecture of the house and its setting. You might, for example, use a hanging lamp in the porch of a period house (not too bright) or contemporary wall lights for a more modern one. Rather than floodlighting the whole house, look at other options such as low-level mood lighting achieved with spiked uplighters in adjacent borders and along pathways. Remember that a town or city house with street lighting will require stronger lighting sources than a secluded country home.

Exits are also important: you need to ensure smooth progress from house to garden. Areas immediately outside French windows, such as terraces, require good lighting to make the transition from the brightness within to the darkness outside. If lights are too bright inside, the reflections on the glazing will kill the lighting effects in the garden. Make sure you can control lighting close to exits or windows; by softening them with a dimmer, you can heighten the intensity of light outside.

ROOF TERRACES AND BALCONIES

The smallest of roof terraces can become an important feature of your home, particularly at night. Lighting a roof terrace extends the feeling of space from within to without, even at times of year when it is not in use. Planters can be lit by low-voltage and LED fittings, concealed behind pots and other containers. For a contemporary effect, coloured lighting can be positioned to 'wash' walls, accentuating their texture and providing drama at night that can be changed.

The pergola posts are dramatically up and downlit with up/downlights mounted at a high level.

PLAN LIGHTING EARLY

Lighting should never be an afterthought; it should be an element of the design that is apparent from the beginning. It is far more practical to deal with unsightly cabling when trenches are being dug for other garden works than to have to think of ways to conceal it retrospectively. If cables are to be buried, make sure that they are at a depth at which they will not be disturbed when you are digging the garden over. They need to be specially armoured or carried within a conduit to ensure they are sealed. All connections must be in waterproof housing and breakers fitted so that power is cut off if water gets into the system.

Lighting is an ingredient on which it is worth spending money from the beginning – not just in terms of having trenches built, but buying the best fittings you can. Most light fittings for the garden are black, but where possible buy dark green, as these blend with the colour of garden foliage. Copper is also effective, as it takes on a greenish patina with age.

Do take maintenance into account when choosing fittings. Any garden fitting will have a protective glass cover that will need regular cleaning and should be checked every few months to make sure it has not become submerged by plants and dirt. Regular maintenance ensures lighting effects always perform at their best.

ENERGY CONSUMPTION

In the past couple of years, the way a garden can be lit eco-consciously has changed dramatically. This is because there are very good LED alternatives to conventional halogen lamps available. Any old-fashioned security floodlight is about 200 watts; using LED fittings you could virtually light an entire city garden for that. LED fittings cost more but can reduce energy consumption to around one-twentieth of what it might otherwise have been, so saving a great deal of money in the long term. However, be warned. There are many cheap LED fittings flooding the market, and these will give only a slight marker light as opposed to a proper effect. Buy only from reputable suppliers who will guarantee the products they sell.

Low energy costs are not the only advantage of LED fittings. They tend to come in smaller casings, so are ideal for compact spaces, such as individual steps. They are also slightly whiter than a regular tungsten light, so when reflected off greenery they give a silvery, moonlight effect which is very pretty. Whereas halogen lights have transformers, LEDs have similar boxes called drivers. These have the advantage that they can be further away from the LEDs than a transformer can be from a halogen lamp.

There is no doubt that the future of lighting design lies with LEDs. As each year goes by, more and more excellent LED fittings become available. They can be used to light the garden beautifully while saving significant amounts of energy and therefore money. The LED revolution allows us all to do our bit for the planet and still enjoy a magical garden.

Sally Storey

LEFT ABOVE AND BELOW:
The magic of this London garden at night is created through various focuses, including the water feature, loggia and the change of levels. The garden is lit like an external room with minimal energy consumption, using the latest LED technology.
RIGHT (clockwise from top left): Copper starlighters work well suspended in a tree to provide soft points of light. They are best hung in threes, fives or sevens (depending on the size of the tree).
Miniature 1W LED Sienna steplights are used to light the steps softly.
Small LEDs uplight the dramatic, stainless-steel water feature.
The drama of the lit water feature is a focus at the end of the garden.

GARDEN | RANDLE SIDDELEY

OPPOSITE: The character of the autumnal garden is emphasised when the structure of the shrubs are highlighted. Directional steplights are used to give a discreet wash to the steps. Downlighters are used on the trellis to throw pools of light on to the lawn.

LEFT: Recessed uplights catch the movement of the water.

FOLLOWING PAGES: This wonderful courtyard demonstrates how successfully the external lighting can work in conjunction with the internal lighting.

PAGES 220–21: This elegant hotel roof terrace is the perfect viewpoint for the city. The dramatic up/downlight on each post provides the ambient light. Under the perimeter banquets, an LED ropelight gives a soft wash of light which reflects off the stone. Just out of view is a dramatic bar incorporating a colour-changing water feature, and adjusting the colour of this strongly affects the ambient mood of the terrace.

INDEX

Frances Lincoln Limited
4 Torriano Mews
Torriano Avenue
London NW5 2RZ
www.franceslincoln.com

Garden
Copyright © Frances Lincoln Limited 2011
Text copyright © Randle Siddeley 2011
Helen Chislett retains the right to be recognised as author of the text.
Photographs copyright © 2011 Randle Siddeley with the exception of those listed
below.

The author is grateful to the following for permission to reproduce photographs
on the following pages:
    Marianne Majerus: 4, 136, 137, 139, 140, 141, 211, 214 and 215
    Homes & Gardens: 186–7
    Katherine Pooley Ltd: 11, 122 and 123
    Beit Salahieh Hotel, Aleppo, Syria: 49, 68, 69, 70, 71, 72–3, 212, 218–19, 220
    and 221;
and to Colin Philp, for supplying transparencies for pages 2, 6, 8–9, 12–21, 75–9,
80–85, 90, 93–115, 124–8, 168–71, 172–4, 184–5, 188–91, 196–7, 199–203, 213
and 224.

First Frances Lincoln edition 2011

A catalogue record for this book is available from the British Library.

ISBN 9780711230781

Printed and bound in China

1 2 3 4 5 6 7 8 9

Miniature box topiary echoes the mature topiary in the background.